Awaken to Love

A Heart & Soul Approach to a Better Love Relationship

Dr. Charlotte Howard

Deep Eddy Works
Austin, Texas

Copyright © 2008 by Charlotte Howard, Ph.D.

Deep Eddy Works
508 Deep Eddy Avenue
Austin, TX 78703

All rights reserved. May not be reproduced without publisher's written permission.

ISBN: 978-0-9816137-0-3

Printed in the United States of America

This book is warmly dedicated to all those who are brave enough to choose Love even when it is difficult.

~ Charlotte Howard

CONTENTS

Part 1: Relationships Are Worth It

Chapter 1: A Psychological Perspective: Physiology & Attachment   13

Chapter 2: A Spiritual Perspective: Knowing The Divine Through Your Relationship   21

    Using Pain for Growth   23
    A Mirror to Know Yourself   26
    The Gifts of Commitment   27

Part 2: Healing Pain & Separation: The Return to Love

Chapter 3: Healing Yourself   31

    Self-Responsibility   34
    Feeling Fully   38
    Injury Meets Love   41
    Facing the Present Reality   44
    What We Resist Persists   50

Claims on Existence	51
Projections	55
Humor & Mercy	57
Involving Your Beloved	59

Chapter 4: Healing Your Beloved — 65

Beware of the Elicited Response	66
Containment & Remembrance	69
Identifying the Medicine	72
Delivering the Medicine	74
Meeting the Feeling	81
Being the Earth	83

Chapter 5: Healing Your Relationship — 85

Teamwork & Goodwill	86
Attributions	87
Being Right or in Relationship	89
Facts vs. Feelings	90
The Power of Roles	92
Step by Step	100
Intentions & Mistakes	102
Connection on Subtle Levels	104
Game Plan	107

Part 3: Simple Techniques For Lasting Love

Chapter 6: Communicate Effectively — 113

Ambiguity is the Enemy — 114
Verbal & Nonverbal Communication — 118
Exploring vs. Explaining — 121
Navigating Similarity & Difference — 122
Slowing It Down — 126

Chapter 7: Water Your Tree — 131

Being Known — 131
Acceptance — 134
Discernment — 139
Neediness — 141
The Dance of Closeness & Separation — 143
Cognitions & Context — 146
Key Moments — 148
Responsiveness — 150
Banishing Boredom — 155
The Role of Ritual — 159
Your Inner Male & Female — 164
Layers of the Heart — 166

Introduction

Awaken to Love combines the wisdom from spiritual and psychological approaches to powerfully transform and enrich the love between partners. I wrote this book for spiritual people, of any religion or spiritual path, who are ready to heal or deepen a committed relationship. I draw on my experience as a psychologist, a wife, and a spiritual seeker with background in Christianity and the heart-centered, mystical tradition of Sufism. The spiritual concepts explored are based on our common threads, such as love for the Divine and commitment to bringing God's caring, compassion, and love to each other, the world, and ourselves. When I use terms such as Love (with a capital "L" to refer to God), you may want to substitute the word for the Divine that is most meaningful to you.

The first of Awaken to Love's three sections, "Relationships Are Worth It," provides the context for the hard work ahead by exploring the profound importance and role in our lives of a committed relationship. The second section, "Healing Pain & Separation: The Return to Love," guides you in bringing healing and peace to the existing pain, conflict, and problems that have built up in your relationship, and gives you a system for resolving future issues that arise.

Inner healing is a necessary foundation on which to build the strong, fulfilling relationship you want. The third section of <u>Awaken to Love</u>, "Simple Techniques for Lasting Love," provides the secrets for building and deepening so that you can realize and maintain the love and support that will feed both you and your beloved throughout your lives.

Section One

Relationships Are Worth It

Chapter One

A Psychological Perspective: Physiology & Attachment

"In the Name of Love She called Her Lover
He returned the call encircling the meanings She carried
And He saw his Destiny in Unity...
Something holy from Her eye lights the darkness of the night
It is the Light and the brilliant connection of the Light...
He encircles Her and She encircles Him
Beauty has displayed Its meaning[i]"

Relating to others defines the human experience. We are social animals, with a deep drive to connect. Similar to eating, drinking, and finding safety, connecting with those around us is also an essential ingredient to survival and growth. Yes, relationships are a source of richness and beauty in our lives, but many people are amazed to realize how deeply programmed we are to be dependent—both joyfully and painfully—on human connection. This dependence is both psychological and biological, in a manner that reaches across the various systems of our bodies. Understanding the vital nature of relationships on this physiological level will create a foundation for the central healing and love-building processes we will explore later. We must at least understand why we bother with intimate relationships when they are so complex, require so much energy, and stimulate so many turbulent feelings. This brief chapter will look at how we are created to require connection from infancy for our basic self-regulation and brain development and how early care can affect future relationships. It is the most research-oriented chapter, and some people may prefer to skip ahead to the more personal second chapter.

In the early 1900's, researchers noticed that orphan children in foundling homes had become listless due to lack of social stimulation. Most of them died because their immune systems and self-regulating brain centers could not develop properly with the lack of touch they were experiencing. Those who lived were socially and emotionally disabled for life. Harlow's[ii] 1973 studies with baby monkeys demonstrated that the drive for contact can be stronger than the drive for physical sustenance. At a basic level the provision of touch and intimate contact with others in development means life or death—our bodies are created to depend on it for the formation of adequate body functioning. Additionally, early touch affects a large number of other important variables, such as the ability to regulate emotions, have a coherent sense of self, and function interpersonally.

Brain research now shows that an infant's early experiences with its caregivers have profound effects on who the person becomes and how he or she will function as an adult. As infants, our brains are in a state of potential. Daniel Siegel, M.D.,[iii] an eminent researcher and professor at UCLA, maps the powerful impacts of various parental relational behaviors on a child's brain development. He and others have shown repeatedly that connections in the limbic region of the brain are destroyed or strengthened based on the baby's emotions and the presence or lack of external soothing.

We maintain significant brain plasticity throughout life, but an infant's brain is extremely malleable, simply waiting for experiences to maintain, strengthen or form important neurological connections, or selectively weed out existing ones through disuse or harmful conditions, such as too much stress. Similar to a child's propensity for learning languages, learning potentials connected to human relationships make some relational skills much easier to acquire very early in life than later. If the infant is deprived of attuned emotional responses, he or she will likely fail to develop basic capacities for emotional regulation and attunement with others. The emotional bond between infant and caregiver that allows for the development of these important abilities is formed in large part through physical contact, affection, and emotional attunement (a parent's ability to sensitively attend to his or her child's needs for soothing and physical care).

Collaborative interactions in which the child "feels felt" by the caregiver are important. The infant must experience a nonverbal, emotional sharing with the caregiver to eventually develop sensitivity to the feelings, thoughts, and perceptions of others. Extreme cases of intrusive or neglectful parenting can produce autism-like symptoms. Siegel emphasizes that the neurological circuits responsible for social perception which develop through contact with the caregiver also regulate emotions, the creation of meaning, the ability to communicate interpersonally, and the organization of memory.

==A caregiver's responses to an infant create long-lasting effects on how that individual expects to be treated by others and how he or she perceives others.== In the case of child abuse, for instance, the brain learns to anticipate danger in connecting with others and is more susceptible to a life-long sense of vulnerability and terror. For example, abused children have elevated baseline and reactive stress hormone levels because of the destructive way the abuse affects the development of the hypothalamic-pituitary-adrenocortical (HPA) axis, a part of the brain that plays an important role in responding to stress.

Rhawn Joseph, Ph.D.,[iv] a prominent brain researcher and a founder of the field of developmental neuropsychology, describes how the limbic functioning of the brain is affected by parenting, where unhealthy contact or lack of contact from others can lead to atrophy or seizure-like over-stimulation of certain brain areas. For instance, over-stimulation of the amygdala can cause extreme desire for others, whereas over-stimulation of the septal nucleus over-corrects the amygdala's arousal and leaves the person desiring a high level of social withdrawal. We all have our preferences for different levels of closeness and separation, and understanding that these can be largely physiological

A PHYSIOLOGICAL PERSPECTIVE

may help us be more compassionate with our partners when our needs conflict with theirs.

Similarly, the right hemisphere of the brain, which develops more actively during the first two years of life and is therefore more affected by early life experience, is responsible for stress-coping responses (such as self-soothing), the development of identity, and the regulation and communication of emotion. According to neuropsychologist Allan Schore[v], faculty in the UCLA Department of Psychiatry and Biobehavioral Sciences, the right hemisphere is especially dependent on attachment experiences to mature properly. The right hemisphere learns to modulate the duration and intensity of feelings through the caregiver's attunement, organizing the chaotic connections that exist at birth and helping regulate emotional and bodily information from the outside. In a way, we continue doing this for each other to some extent throughout life.

Schore talks about how the right hemisphere is also key in having a unified sense of self and a coherent autobiographical story. Therefore, children who were not able to attach to their parents and receive sufficient contact often do not have an integrated sense of self that spans their life. Because some brain plasticity exists through adulthood, psychotherapy can foster connections in this part of the brain through helping clients develop this self-narrative and through providing the reflection of themselves back to them that they never received as children. Particularly in long-term group therapy, people become able to better know and express what they are feeling and understand who they are in relationships, changing themselves at a neurological level. Through this process people can develop the possibility of connecting more with other people emotionally.

As adults we can be triggered, in situations of felt terror or rage, into regressed states in which the integrative functioning of the prefrontal regions are impaired. Siegel describes how in these situations the brain may have little communication between emotional states/impulses and rational/reflective processes because the limbic system is not connecting with the more-evolved cortex. This kind of emotional flooding is much more frequent and severe for those with insecure attachments from childhood or with histories of trauma, but is possible for all of us under certain stress conditions. Learning what these conditions are for us and our partners is important. In these situations we must be caring with people because their brains may not have the resources to function adaptively in that moment.

Understanding human connection from a biological or physiological point of view can give us insight into our partner's (and our own) "crazy" behavior and make it less overwhelming. We can stay curious and open to learning how to care for each other in these places of need. Being a secure base for one another, both in the moment and over time, has a powerful effect on people and can change attachment patterns over time. Research shows[vi] that a person with an attachment problem is likely to no longer have the problem after only four years of marriage to a person who does not have an attachment problem. So, profound neurological changes can happen if we have

A PHYSIOLOGICAL PERSPECTIVE

patience and the right re-parenting through psychotherapy or other prolonged healthy relationships. We can learn to think of our partner's need for soothing like any other physical need—in the same way that feeding people dinner affects their bodies, holding them emotionally stabilizes them neurologically.

In summary, the functioning of our brains is very much affected by the frequency and quality of our contact with others. Engaging in long-term relationships is not just for fun, it is a fundamental aspect of our life experience and developmental process. Our relationships can be a safe haven and source of strength. A spiritual perspective might hold that the Divine literally built our beings to need love, both directly from Him, and through other humans, from day one when our immune system and nervous system cannot develop properly without it, to adulthood when our dependence on caring surfaces regularly, particularly under stress. Love and affection are clearly a key part of this holy journey on earth. Through our need for soothing, we learn to receive. This understanding may equip us with the motivation and commitment for the difficult work of creating a relationship that is fulfilling in the deepest ways.

Chapter Two

A Spiritual Perspective: Knowing the Divine Through Your Relationship

"The understanding of God and all that His love means to you is completed by the sharing of the deep secret love with another. It is putting the essence of all the teachings, all the books, all the sciences, and all that God has given to you into manifestation through the love you share with your beloved.[vii]*"*

People long for intimacy and connection, even if they defend against this desire and appear to repel closeness. As described in the previous chapter, healthy relationships and physical contact are critical to our physiological development and continue to be physically and emotionally stabilizing throughout life. They also bring joy and the important experience of being known and understood. Life experiences seem more satisfying and enjoyable if you have someone with whom to share them. Those without relationships have the sometimes difficult, but vital, task of learning how to shift from being "alone" to being "with oneself." People can be with themselves in a fulfilling and meaningful way that will take the edge off of loneliness and facilitate personal growth. Perhaps the loneliest feeling, in fact, is feeling alone when you are with someone. How to be with these feelings will be addressed in the following chapters. When functioning as they should, however, relationships make life richer and feed our spirits deeply because of the sense of support and being known.

In addition to happiness and companionship, committed romantic relationships have profound spiritual meaning and purpose. Relationships facilitate personal growth and development through both love and pain. In their good moments, relationships allow people to feel unconditionally loved and supported in a way that heals the deep pain of past experiences in which love was not available from others in the right ways. It heals insecurities about who one is and whether or not one is lovable and acceptable. In this case, it is not surprising that relationships feel completing, as though one's whole being sighs with relief and relaxes into the love of the beloved.

This love is a portal to Divine Love. As we trust our partners we can travel beyond human love and into the arms of God, remembering the complete Love that lives in the deepest place in our hearts. When we are in the feeling of love and being loved, we are already touching the part of our hearts that knows God. Swimming in that love, and becoming it, is only a step away. It requires not stopping with your lover, but going inside and beyond to the source of that Love. This step is an act of surrendering our beings into the qualities of God, and knowing that it is God who is the Love and the Companion. Whatever we experience of these qualities in the world is a taste of God's unimaginably vast and complete caring for us.

When one beloved gives a holy quality, such as love or compassion, to the other, the other often returns it ten-fold, which inspires the beloved to give even more, and so the process continues into deeper and deeper states of love and generosity. This process is perhaps the easiest way to reach God-realization. The holiness builds into the complete knowledge and trust of the Divine, until we allow ourselves to be nothing else—seeing everything through the lens of compassion and caring. At some point in surrendering and merging with our beloveds and the Beloved, we let go of "I" and only the Love exists, so we dissolve into God and return to Unity with Him. A story of one spiritual master describes how he would not accept a new student who wanted to know God if the student had never loved. The teacher told the student to return after learning to have love for anything, even if it was a donkey.

Using Pain for Growth

Spiritual walking through love begetting love and generosity begetting generosity is easy and beautiful. Few people, however, reach God only through the experience of beauty. Most people's hearts are veiled with layers and layers of hurt and painful beliefs that separate us from complete love and cause us to do and witness (give our attention to) things that thwart its growth in our hearts or the hearts of our beloveds. The path to God is both through surrendering in the love and beauty, and also through surrendering in the suffering and conflict. We must wash our hearts of the veils and illusions by allowing Love to touch each one. This process can be difficult because we tightly guard these vulnerable places within us. At some point these defenses functioned for our protection, when we did not fully know how to receive Divine protection. When we try to release them, the painful pictures and voices will resist because they are familiar and have served us in some way.

For instance, the belief that people cannot be trusted may have been learned from one's unavailable mother, and then this picture prevented getting close to others who might also be untrustworthy and cause more pain. It feels as if the stakes are high—we might die if we let go of these illusions, partly because of the vulnerability underneath that we must face, and partly because we do not know who we are or what the world would be like without them, creating a loss of control. I have many clients in my psychology practice who have shut down their feelings so much that they do not know how they feel and their partners complain that they are cold or unavailable. These clients must understand how adaptive closing their hearts was when they were younger and living in abusive or harsh families. It was then safer not to feel, so this defense becomes a best friend—familiar and vital to emotional survival. Yet, as adults, they must do the difficult work of letting this defense go so that they can have

A SPIRITUAL PERSPECTIVE

meaningful relationships and a fulfilling life experience. Partners force us to face places inside us such as these, and help us to wash them, whether by loving us or by rubbing against the painful spots until we look at them.

The process of healing will be described in detail in the following chapters. For now it is simply important to note that a central purpose of relationships is to show us where we need more love and where we have trouble giving love, receiving love, or staying in the love. Essentially, committed long-term relationships can bring up our issues more than almost anything else. It is through this process of being triggered with no escape (besides leaving a meaningful relationship) that we have the opportunity to heal the things that separate us from the Divine. A spiritual master is one who has no objection to any state in which God puts him/her. What better way to find out which states we object to than being in a relationship!

Anyone in a relationship will find many, many things that feel intolerable and impossible to bear. Discovering these places is a jewel in the spiritual journey because it shows us where we do not trust God and where we lose sight of His ability to suffice us (be enough for us) in any state. Through relationships we witness parts of ourselves daily that need healing and washing with love. I often have clients who tell me: "I only act that way with my partner," or "She/he is the only one who can make me that angry." Relationships flush up all the most injured and ugly places in us (in addition to all the most beautiful). If you take the time to clean these places as they arise, you are on a very fast track to deep holiness, peace, and beauty in your life. Our spiritual walking and personal growth can be so clear and fast if we use pain as a door.

A Mirror to Know Yourself

Your beloved is a mirror to reflect back to you who you are. On the outer it can happen when you find yourself being less than loving because you were susceptible to being triggered by your beloved's behavior. Here you witness a part of yourself that is unloving, or able to lose the love because of an outer circumstance. Certain aspects of your beloved and his/her behavior allow you to see your own pain and difficulty. For example, without someone there to leave a mess all over your kitchen or bedroom, how would you know how easy it is to upset your sense of peace and well-being? Or, if your beloved is not listening, you may be able to see and feel the part of you that has always felt unattended to. This process of seeing what is stirred up in you by the relationship is how you know yourself through your beloved.

The beloved is also a mirror in a more subtle way. With my husband, for instance, the way in which I relate to him within myself is almost always reflected back to me by his behavior and how it feels to be around him. I may appear to be the perfect wife on the outside, doing and saying all the right things, but if I am angry with him inside, he will usually keep his distance from me. In this case his distance mirrors to me a part of myself of which I may not be aware. When I see his distance, I have the opportunity to feel in my heart what might be keeping him away, and then, in this case, I can become aware of my anger and have the opportunity to explore and work through it. Generally, when I spend time with a feeling and begin healing it within myself rather than sending it his way, he will immediately shift his behavior. In fact, repeatedly, the moment I make this inner shift he will call my name from the other side of the house because he suddenly desires to be close to me. So, you have an amazing opportunity to discover unconscious feelings or aspects of yourself just by using your beloved's feelings and actions as a mirror for who you are within yourself and who you are in relationship.

The Gifts of Commitment

This process can be much safer and deeper within a long-term, committed relationship. Commitment provides a container in which to move through difficult times and grow to be a more complex, fulfilled person. Engaging in a series of short-term relationships is similar to reliving your teenage years over and over, repeatedly reworking the same developmental tasks and experiences. Though every relationship is different, the range of experiences can be limited in terms of depth, as one never finds out what the relationship would be like in twenty years. In general, relationships follow a developmental process where lust decreases over time, and outer romance and the passionate "in love" feeling are almost always muted or gone within two to four years. The attachment and deep love between two people, however, increases throughout the course of a relationship. This attachment, as described previously in relation to the brain's capacity for connection, can be one of the most profound and healing human experiences, only growing richer with time. Being together through the pain, the beauty, and all that life brings over time, seems to create a depth and maturation similar to the aging of a fine wine.

==Commitment to a partner is also a commitment to oneself. Making a choice to have a long-term relationship is like promising to go through the full range of human experience and thereby know and accept many subtle, yet-undiscovered, aspects of oneself.== To weather the difficulty that will inevitably arise in relationships, one must meet and walk through the painful places within oneself. Often giving up on relationships is giving up on oneself—not being able to tolerate the places inside that are stimulated by the relationship, places that could be healed if we do not run away. So, as this journey of relationship brings both pain and joy, one must know how to facilitate growth through the pain, and also how to build the love in the relationship to protect and nurture the joy, comfort, and fulfillment it offers. The remaining two sections of this book will explore these two key aspects of insuring that your heart is nurtured by your relationship.

Section Two

Healing Pain & Separation: The Return to Love

Chapter Three

Healing Yourself

"Then plant your tree. Put the seed back into your earth, water it with...the essence of love...and let it grow up in the light of knowing....When the tree is grown, keep this tree inside you. Then sit under it and take a branch in your hand, and take the fruit from the branch of the milk of the essence of the love. By eating this you begin to live, and in so giving birth to yourself, you unearth the holy treasure that He created you to bear. Then when you look into the treasure with the eye of your soul, you see One Who sees you looking into the essence of the jewel. God sees you as you see Him. Look again. There is no you, only He. It is He Who sees Himself in the mirror of your soul, as it remembers itself in the treasure of His essence. Then, in truth, you live in the garden of love...[viii]"

One theory about how humans change[ix] holds that the most effective way to reach our goals is to weaken the restraining forces (what holds us back), rather than by increasing our effort to move toward the goal. If you take the roadblocks out of the way, our life energy naturally moves us forward. So, "trying harder" is not always the easiest way. This model compares people to Sisyphus, from ancient Greek mythology, who had to push a large boulder up a hill and when it reached the top it would always roll back down so that he would have to start again. His life was spent pushing this rock up hill for eternity. If he pushed harder, the rock might move up more quickly, but as soon as he stopped pushing it would roll back down. Similarly, we can try to push through our issues, but we spend a lot of energy that way, and backslide as soon as we become tired and stop trying as ardently. A more efficient way of addressing our concerns is to remove the obstacles—in our analogy, decreasing the size of the rock or the slope of the hill. To remove or decrease the restraining forces in a relationship might involve healing the wounds or beliefs people have that fuel their problems.

For example, someone may try hard to find the right woman to make him feel loved, dating one woman after another until she disappoints him and he moves on. Instead of putting more effort into finding the "right" woman, he might do better to focus on lowering his defenses against feeling loved by another. His "receiver" may be tuned to the wrong frequency to protect him from finding a woman who would give him reason to open his heart, which he fears would hurt him as it did as a child.

One man was a relatively happy infant until his sickly sister was born and all the family's attention went to her. During her many hospitalizations and operations, his parents were absent and he was left with a depressed aunt who was very critical of him. He learned to close his heart to lessen

HEALING YOURSELF

the pain. As an adult he hungered for the connection he had as an infant, but could not open to receive love unless the woman treated him "perfectly." In particular, he would always find some experience where he felt abandoned, and would then leave the relationship. What are the Sisyphus rocks that you are constantly pushing against or carrying around inside? In this chapter we will look at how to address these deep issues within you.

Every person feels painful emotions from time to time. When these feelings occur often, however, and your beloved appears to be the cause of your feelings, the love between the two of you may become taxed and begin to deteriorate. Many relationships are destroyed by negative feelings and the belief that one's partner cannot or will not meet one's needs. It is vital, then, to have a way to effectively process and heal one's wounds and return to a loving position in which the relationship can grow and has a better chance of nurturing both people. Though talking to your beloved about your feelings can be a great way to clear the air and encourage healthy communication, which is a lifeline, your beloved may not have the skills or emotional health (at least around certain issues) to respond in a way that facilitates your feeling better. He or she may become defensive, angry, or hurt in response to your feelings, rather than showing the care and empathy that would create healing and closeness. Many people give up at that point and over time become hopeless about receiving what they desire. Let's look at how we can return to Love without another person's help.

When you are feeling sadness, anger, or fear in your relationship, you have an opportunity for making enormous personal and spiritual growth. In fact, many people have reached God-realization primarily or solely through walking through the issues that come up in their lives, rather than through spiritual practices, religious services, etc. This way of spiritual growth is rapid because we return to God each place in our being that does not know love as soon as we become aware of it, allowing light to conquer darkness in our lives every time the feeling of separation and pain appears. Eventually, we <u>become</u> God's qualities and nothing inside resists what God places before us.

Self-Responsibility

The first step is self-responsibility. Self-responsibility allows you to shift your focus from your partner to yourself so that you can begin to heal what is stirred up inside you. Self-responsibility is becoming response-able, able to respond in a useful way. You cannot heal yourself while looking outside yourself. We all tend to look externally to find causes for our feelings and answers to the problems. This outward focus often leads us into expending a lot of energy outside ourselves to change the perceived problem, which is either wasted effort because the outside will not change, or we "fix" the problem only to have the same feelings about other external stimuli. This cycle is discouraging and tiring, leading many people to feel out of control and even more determined to gain control by

HEALING YOURSELF

mastering their environment or situation. The process is endless and even during those wonderful times when everything goes right, we unfortunately continue carrying inside the original issues that will sooner or later be triggered once again.

Self-responsibility allows us to bypass this fruitless process so that we can explore and heal our internal landscape, which creates lasting change in our experience of life and love. One spiritual teacher[x] said: "Why try to walk so that the thorn in your foot does not hurt so much, or build a shoe that mitigates the pain from the thorn? Instead, pull out the thorn!" This shift is critical, but far easier said than done! To move your attention from the outside to the inside, you must remember that your experience in relationship is never about the other person, and always about something in you that needs love and completion. Whatever your partner's behavior, your interpretations and reactions are what create your experience. Many people are unable to take this step to looking at themselves, especially in the moment of strong emotions. Everything in you will say that it is your partner's fault or that if the situation would change you would be okay. In truth, responsibility for conflicts or dynamics in relationships lies with both partners. The jewel for you, your growth, and your happiness, however, is in the part that is about you.

It may even feel as though you would die if you let go of your tenacious hold on your conviction that someone or something is wrong and must change. In a way part of you does die when you make this shift—the part of you that is caught in suffering about this issue. The objection that part of you is voicing through these strong feelings is its only claim on existence. It will die if it receives love here. In fact, the issue will already begin to die if you shift to the belief that the pain could leave without the external situation changing. You will see how tangible this experience is when you try to make the shift to self-responsibility yourself next time you are having a strong reaction to your beloved. It may feel almost impossible to stop thinking about the outer stimulus that "caused" the feelings, and instead look at your own heart and what is moving inside you apart from any supposed external cause.

The beauty of this major step is that you put yourself in a position to grow, and you reclaim true freedom in that you are not trapped by the voices that make the situation about something out of your control. Taking self-responsibility does not mean that your beloved does not have his/her part in whatever is causing you pain. Instead, it means that the part your beloved plays is irrelevant to you during this first step of returning to the love within. Your goal is self-healing, so you must be looking at yourself (and God, of course). Tomorrow your beloved may change the behavior, feeling, or belief that makes you so hurt or angry, and then you would have lost the chance to heal this part of yourself, at least until it surfaces again in relation to something else. But in the meantime you are stuck carrying around this issue or vulnerability, because now your beloved has changed so that it is no longer triggered and brought to the surface for healing. Later, once you are in the wisdom of the Love

HEALING YOURSELF

inside, you can make a good decision about how to handle the outer situation. So by looking at yourself first you do not miss your chance to increase your inner peace and beauty.

Some bring up extreme examples to challenge this approach, such as, "What if your partner is physically abusive?" Of course in this situation your first step must be to find physical safety. Then, however, it is all the more useful and critical to spend time looking only at yourself, not blaming anyone or anything outside, so that you can heal the issues that brought you to an abusive situation in the first place. If you can return to the love for the beloved underneath the abuser, and leave the relationship because it is the wise thing to do rather than from anger or desperation, you are much less likely to repeat the pattern and end up in another abusive relationship, or return to the original relationship.

If, for instance, your underlying issue is hating yourself and that is why you have chosen someone who reflects this image back to you, then if you leave the relationship you are likely only to find another partner who makes you feel just as awful. It is actually the self-hatred that makes you feel bad, not simply the way that hatred manifests in your relationships. In fact, if you can look in your heart and really love the places of anger and hurt in the process that will be described, you may heal the underlying issues deeply enough so that when you leave the relationship, you are really free.

So, taking self-responsibility is almost always a step toward empowerment and wholeness. Feelings that come up in relationship show you what needs to be cleaned or healed inside, even if you are "right" to be angry or hurt. If you are not in the Love (able to access the love and peace within, and even direct it toward your beloved), then you are the one who needs your attention first and who needs to shift inside—for your own sake! The hurt self will say it is vital to tell your partner what needs to change and nothing exists for which you can take responsibility. A good way to discern whether or not you should believe this voice and go directly to giving your partner feedback, is if your feedback will only come from love for your partner and be for your partner's own use in helping him/her progress toward wholeness. If you pass this test, go for it! If not, you are ready to look at yourself first. Once your focus is internal, rather than on your situation or your partner, the healing process has begun.

Feeling Fully

Healing occurs when the injury you have been carrying inside for who knows how long comes in contact with Love, and the other qualities of God, such as Mercy, Compassion, and Patience. So, the healing process has two critical aspects: feeling one's feelings fully and holding one's feelings in a loving way, which is actually letting God touch those places. If you have shifted from blame to self-responsibility, you have already taken the most important step in feeling one's feelings fully. For example, if you find yourself berating your partner in your head, or lecturing him/her, or complaining, then you are defending against actually feeling what is happening inside. You may

HEALING YOURSELF

feel the anger or hurt in the periphery, as all the voices in your head come from this pain (trying to fix the situation, get even, be understood, etc.), but this way of feeling allows you to stay in your mind and avoid truly sinking into the raw feelings in your heart. This human tendency is a trick, because it is much more painful and toxic to be on the outside of feelings and acting them out in one's mind, than to just feel what is actually present. Unfortunately, over the years we have developed the habit of defending against this primary experience and evading the place that really needs attention. This process replicates the early experiences we had of our pain being neglected.

When you catch yourself avoiding feelings in this way, or some other way, you might take some time alone and place your hand on the center of your chest. Feel yourself sinking in and giving space to whatever physical sensations and emotions are moving in your heart. Gently open and continue falling into the rawness of whatever is. For me, I can be grumpy and tense for several hours, but as soon as I pause to place my hand on my heart and be fully present, I begin to cry. If you know there is nothing wrong with anything you feel, it is paradoxically less painful to cry out in pain than to walk around generally anxious or upset with the sense that something is not right.

When you begin to fully feel whatever is present for you, your mind may try to distract you from the pure emotion by returning to blaming your partner or whatever upset you and planning how to handle it. Another trick that may appear self-responsible, but really takes you away from looking at yourself, is trying to understand your partner's perspective. Though that may be more compassionate than blaming and judging, you will still end up avoiding what was stimulated in you. You may never be able to understand the other's perspective, or to fully see as acceptable that another person has a different perspective or could do something like *that*, but it is more productive to feel your own pain about how impossible and intolerable that seems, than to try to figure it out. Ultimately it is good to try to understand the other person, but first comes your own healing, and your mind will try to take you in many other directions to avoid this turning inward and to God.

To prevent these distractions from hindering your own healing and honoring of your experience and its deeper significance, try looking beyond the outside to the core feeling. For instance, you might be thinking: "That is so wrong for him to say that to me. I can't believe it. That is so mean," or "How could she do that? What was going through her mind?" Instead, shift to your underlying experience: "I don't feel loved," or "I feel alone," without attaching that to your beloved or any one event—just the deep pain of that human emotion which probably has thousands of stories in your life that inform how it feels for you personally.

Also, it is okay if you do not feel much as you begin to take time to honor your core feelings and your heart. Just be with whatever you do feel. Perhaps your heart just feels tight and closed. Being with that feeling of tightness is still preferable to ignoring it and pushing through with your day. Always acknowledge what is real rather than try to create something you think should be. For instance, "I thought I was furious, but now that I go inside my heart all I feel is openness and stillness." Rather than try to find what you imagine you feel, just sink gently in and softly open to discover what is actually your present experience inside your body.

Injury Meets Love

Once you have created space to feel your raw emotions, you are ready for the next step of healing, which has to do with how you relate to these feelings. James Keeley, spiritual teacher and healer, and author of *Walking With God*[xi], suggests imagining your feeling is a little child who was running happily and then suddenly tripped and skinned his knee. The child's face contorts with pain and he comes screaming and crying to you, his loving parent. Be with your feeling and present experience exactly as you would be with that child: embrace it with love; comfort and soothe it. You might say slowly and softly to the self as you hold it in your arms and stroke its back: "Oh, beloved, this hurts so much! Ouch! This is so hard. It will be okay. Just let it out." You are not trying to make the self stop feeling what it is feeling, you are simply being with your experience in a comforting, holding, loving way. You are honoring yourself and your emotions. An ignored feeling will act just as an ignored child, endlessly tugging at your pant leg, saying "Pay attention to me!" until you give it love and compassion.

Connecting your pain with love is opening the pain to be healed by the real Lover—God. Whenever you feel the tender, holding, merciful presence described above in the image of the loving parent with the hurt child, you have merely made space to allow God to move in you, or to remember the love that is already present and available to you from Him. In fact, holding your emotions in this loving way is only a door to really receive from the fullness of God's qualities and to allow yourself, and your pain, to be fully held in the complete Love and Wholeness of the Divine. How can we expect to feel the presence of God when we are relating to ourselves in such a different way than the Divine does?

When we relate to ourselves with God's qualities, it is He that is relating to us. The more the place of anger, hurt, or fear can taste that Presence, the more it will return to peace and be healed. This process may take time, however, as the place may not trust Love fully right away. Be patient and let it drink it in as much as possible each time the feeling arises, even if it can only swallow a few drops of the Love. We cannot feed an infant meat, but if we feed it milk, it will grow up to be able to digest more hearty nourishment over time.

To summarize the basic process, let me give a recent example. I was washing dishes in the kitchen and was very angry at my husband because in that moment I thought I was doing all the work, which certainly was not true, but I believed it right then. I was talking to him angrily in my head (a great cue that one needs healing!) and telling him how unfair it was, how intolerable it was, and listing all of the things I was doing to help out and all of the things he was not doing. This process of keeping score builds resentment, which is poisonous for relationships. I became increasingly furious as I engaged this internal dialogue. Whenever I would try to stop thinking this way, however, because I thought I should be more loving, I would quickly come back to it without realizing it. Trying to change ourselves does not work any better than trying to change our partners!

I was trying so desperately to be in a loving state and felt so angry at myself for failing. The frustration was only growing. Eventually I remembered to honor my feelings. Anger was more difficult than sadness, because I was judging it as ugly compared to feeling hurt, with which I am more comfortable. As soon as I opened to feel the anger fully, as a raw emotion in me not attached to any particular cause, and then allowed myself to feel compassion for what a difficult experience that was for me, just as I would fully embrace and comfort the child who skinned her knee, I almost immediately felt relieved. I took some deep breaths, soaking up the love, and comfort—feeling how painful it is to be angry at my husband and recognizing that that is okay. It was literally only a few moments after I remembered to give myself love and understanding, rather than passing judgment on myself, even for having a "yucky" feeling like anger, that I effortlessly returned to a loving place inside. I had remembered God and that Love is always available and does not require me to be any certain way to deserve it. I was still washing dishes, but was astonished at how easy it suddenly became and how much satisfaction I was receiving from the idea that I was serving my partner and making things beautiful in our kitchen.

Facing the Present Reality

It does not always happen this quickly. Often I must sit for a half hour or an hour with my raw feelings, while opening to experience how God holds them, before I will feel some peace and relief. Perhaps the most profound mistake we make is trying to change our own state or feelings, rather than experience how God is manifesting in that moment. Veils always exist between us and the complete Reality of God. Though our journey in this life is to walk closer to God by dispelling these illusions that stand in our way one by one, more always exist. The closest veil, however, between us and the reality of God is our present experience because that is the means through which God manifests Himself. Where else can we feel God's presence but in the moment in which we are living? If we avoid the present and the situation and feelings we are being given, we are veiling the veil. In other words, we are moving one step further from experiencing God because we are one step further from where God manifests.

On the other hand, we can quickly return to know Peace if, instead of avoiding the present experience, we practice looking through any feeling or situation to know God and His qualities. In other words, if we open to the present experience, we can observe how He can move us and what He has available to us in that moment. It is tempting to allow God to be the wind moving your sailboat only until the boat glides into rough waters. At that point you may take down your sail because you do not like the direction in which you are headed. Unfortunately, that means you are in rough waters and stuck there because you have disengaged from the reality of what is. Instead, trust God to be the Mover and keep your sail up so that the wind can move you in the way that is best for your spirit, without your human interference or objection. Although you cannot control the direction, at least you are moving and are in the hands of the All-Compassionate. You may know the saying: "When in hell don't stop walking!"

Whatever our experience is, that is what we really want to accept and be present with because it is our means of arrival to God. It is said that the greatest sign of self-reliance (versus relying on God) is discontentment with one's state. So the question is: "How is this situation the nourishment for what my deepest heart wants to become?" Perhaps, for instance, pain in a particular situation provides the opportunity to clean the part that has to have everything a certain way, allowing us to surrender more deeply to God and have real fulfillment.

The only place where we can be sufficed is in the present. You could say, for instance, "Wow, I am needy for God right now!" and open to feel how the Sufficer can move you, which over time leads to knowing yourself, God, and deep contentment because you embrace what is and know God in it. We are created to need the Divine, so that being dependent is right and a very holy state, but many avoid feeling needy at all costs. You may say, "How can I get out of this? Oh, if only I could make her be more affectionate toward me. I could tell her it is over if she does not start x, y, or z." In this case, the pain into which God could send His light is ignored in exchange for a contemplation of a strategy that could change the situation so that you do not need to turn to God for love and support. What if these situations are set up exactly for that purpose—to remind us to turn to the Divine?

In one scenario you choose to allow God to manage your affairs. You then can receive the gifts in life that are far more meaningful than the outer situation. In the other scenario you choose to manage your own affairs and continue searching for an answer to fix this mess and avoid that for which the mess was intended—to lead you to call out to your Beloved, your Creator, to receive sustenance. Calling out to Love to help us is the mysterious place where we can meet the Comforter intimately. Said another way, focusing on worldly ways to fix a problem that could otherwise stimulate our call to God is essentially avoiding the place where we meet God and experience His response. The purpose of turning to God is not to change your situation or state, though you may be asking for or wanting this change and it often naturally happens. The purpose, instead, is to feel God's presence with you in any state or situation and discover and receive how the Divine holds you in that place.

Just as infants regulate their immature systems through contact with the parent's mature systems (e.g., just the presence of the mother in the room can affect the breathing of a sleeping baby), when we surrender completely to God and open for Him to be deeply present with us, we can template our beings from His Truth and Love. We want to merge into Love to have our whole beings filled with a new substance, like a sponge. He can replace our illusions with His Understanding and heal us at any level--down to our cells. It is a matter of present relationship and allowing ourselves to receive and connect. We also tend to go to the past in our minds. Again, the present is where you will find God and His ever-present help. It is where a relationship happens.

We can shift from being in need of things being a certain way to acknowledging our real need for God. To receive and heal we must (1) know we are in trouble and (2) know we do not have what is needed to change it. It is an illusion to think that things can be anything other than what they are in that moment. So, we must accept both what is happening and how we feel about it. Who are we trying to get to surrender to whom if our goal is changing states from the state in which God put us? ==A large part of our pain comes from resistance to what is. Often we've already taken the blow!== For instance, maybe someone says something hurtful to you. Ouch! Now you may want to figure out how to get out of the situation or make sure it does not happen again, or figure out what to do about this person, but you continue to feel upset and hurt. You are stuck! You feel stuck when you can't change things into what you want. So, if God's decree for that moment is not okay with you, you'll be stuck. The fact is, you got hurt. It is too late—it already happened. Avoiding it merely causes the injury to remain there indefinitely. You need to acknowledge the pain and then care for it.

I remember, for instance, when my younger sister got waitlisted at the graduate program I was attending. I was so angry at the professors because she was the perfect candidate, and so disappointed because it threatened our plan for her and her fiancée to move to Iowa to live with me and my fiancée. This moment is one in which I could choose between acting as though I should be in control and engaging in thoughts of how to change the reality, versus accepting what had already happened and opening to discover what would happen next. That was only one scene in the movie—I needed to keep watching and not turn it off because I thought what I saw pointed toward an unhappy ending. We must remember that the hand of Love wrote the script.

As I was crying, my beloved said, trying to get me to smile, "Honey, don't be angry at the admissions committee, if God did not want her to come to this school there wasn't a lot the admissions committee could do about it!" It was not until later, however, that I was able to look back and see the perfect wisdom in the way things happened. The program my sister attended was much better for her than the one I wanted her to attend, but she would not have considered it if she had been accepted right away by my school (to which she did end up being admitted). My first job ended up being a third of the way across the country from my graduate program, but very close to the school my sister chose, and

HEALING YOURSELF

we were able to plan a double wedding and see each other often for the five years that followed, rather than having had one year together in the original location.

Lack of trust and acting as though we have the whole picture leads to needless pain. Rather than pretend to have trust when we don't, however, we must be with the pain and open to see what we are shown or can feel when we connect with something greater than ourselves. In this case feeling God's presence and listening at a deeper level from the beginning would have helped me to surrender more quickly to the way things were going and avoid anger and discontent. Sometimes, however, you may sink into your heart to feel how God holds something and find that you are being asked to act rather than surrender. When this direction comes from the Divine you can feel the Love behind it. Even then, however, if your actions do not create the desired outcomes, you must find trust and acceptance of something larger than yourself because we are not ultimately in control of the way things go.

So, as you engage in self-healing try not to think you know how successful resolution of your pain or the situation would look. Some teachers illustrate this concept by telling the story of a man who was standing at the edge of a cliff trying to muster up the faith to leap. He said: "God, please help me to have the faith to jump!" God replied: "I did not bring you up here to jump, I brought you up here to enjoy the view!" Many times Life puts something before us and we aim for what we think needs to happen as a result, rather than waiting to see what the situation brings up for us and experiencing that. We have a way of making things more difficult than they need to be.

What We Resist Persists

A saying that certainly applies to feelings is: "What we resist persists." Instead of being stuck because you want something to be different, you can call to Love and allow it to respond to your pain and then you can begin to move again because It moves you. Perhaps God even moves you in a better direction than you could have planned. If you are sitting in a stream you may be able to resist the current, but that takes a lot of work and does not make the stream go away. Reality is reality no matter how much we fight it. You may happen to be sitting in the one ugly part of the stream and so you won't let it carry you. If you did, however, you might find a beautiful part around the next bend. And actually, that stream is the only stream in town!! We haven't been given any other life, so we need to engage in this one and not resist what is. In other words, avoiding, resisting or fixing our feelings only perpetuates pain, as the purpose of what we are facing is to help us learn who God is when we are in pain, and that purpose has not yet been served. Borrowing again from James Keeley, a good prayer to have in your heart when you are suffering is: "Oh Beloved God, who are You to me when I am_____(anxious, sad, angry, etc)?"

Whether or not our state changes, which it often does when the Love touches it, we are still in the deeper garden because we feel our connection with the Source of Trust and Patience. When we are upset we must ask how we are witnessing God in that moment. It is said that God reveals Himself wherever we have a good opinion of Him! The only thing that limits us is ignorance of Love—not how someone treats us, or a situation that occurs in our lives. Every pain occurs in a place where God wants to give you more. A series of painful circumstances simply continues to point out a belief you hold about you or your life of which you are ready to let go. Continue asking what each experience introduces you to within yourself. Is that belief or aspect of you emanating from Love? Does it beautify you to hold that belief or way of looking at things? Then open to Love and step out of that world and into God's.

Claims on Existence

Healing is not always easy and you can sometimes feel as though you will die if you let go. As mentioned previously, a part of you does—the attachment to your self (ego) and its beliefs. In some ways this feeling of dying is the height of spiritual walking because it is the place where you face the challenge of surrendering and losing yourself to God. Jesus and many Prophets and spiritual paths tell us to die before we can live, or to die to ourselves, or to die to live in God. For the true spiritual seeker, then, healing is not trying to better the self, it is trying to annihilate it and let God take over!

So, why does it feel like dying to look at oneself and go to the bottom of the pain without blaming it on someone or something outside? Many people stop when they get to this feeling because it is too scary or painful, rather than continuing through it until they are truly free. Pain occurs when we have made a claim on existence ("I am in control" or "Everyone should or is x, y, z", etc) and then discover that it is not true because something happens to challenge it. Rather than let our belief expire because it is not working, we often cling to it and work to reestablish it. Otherwise we would have to face that the self (the ego) may not be the Reality.

The self struggles so vigorously to exist by setting up ideas or pictures and believing them, but it will never be anything but an illusion. So, when an event or relationship challenges this constructed reality, we feel pain—"growing pains" if we surrender to them. We can ask ourselves: "Am I buying or selling?" In other words, I have these feelings, do I want to believe them (buy them) and take them home with me, or would I like to trade them in to God for something else? This question would be easy to answer if it were not for our lack of trust, as well as our attachment to our defenses and our determination to control the world ourselves. For instance, if someone stole from me, I might think trading in my anger for peace means that it is okay for someone to steal from me, or that others will steal from me, or even that I will end up with nothing. So, I had better protect myself from that by continuing to feel angry and focusing on how unacceptable being stolen from is. In reality all I would have accomplished is to deny myself the experience of peace! Feeling peace does not exclude taking action to protect oneself from harm in the future, it merely means you are able to do so in more rational and effective ways without the turbulence from the fear.

The deeper question with which we are faced is: "What do we hang our hat (or our sense of well-being) on?" Does our feeling of being okay depend on the world reflecting our illusions, or is our well-being based on knowing the deeper Truth and allowing our illusions to be destroyed again and again? We must turn in what is temporarily reassuring for what is eternal. All difficult feelings are places where we say "no" to what is. Anger, for instance, is a sign of loss, just as are sadness and fear. Rather than trying to re-create the lost thing, you must feel the feelings of loss, without explaining or understanding, so that the new can come through. This concept is similar to a drop of water claiming it is different from the ocean. When the drop finally returns to the Ocean, it is complete—even though it had to lose itself.

To illustrate, I remember one healing experience that particularly felt like dying. I was dating a man who had difficulty expressing emotion outwardly, and would sometimes push away my physical affection. One time I reached for his hand and he pulled away and continued walking without a word. I had been walking by his side, but I stopped and went in another direction. It hurt my feelings so deeply, and made me so angry, that I could hardly stand it. I had to let go of "standing it," in fact, to truly heal the pain.

By bearing it I could have maintained my existence and not let my "self" be destroyed. Though it still hurt intensely, the feelings were manageable to me as long as I could believe his action was wrong and I had to do something about it (break up with him, ensure it never happened again, etc). It felt manageable only if I could hold onto my picture of what existence and love is or should be. I would not have to change as long as I fought this experience and tried to solve it or bear it.

In the end, however, I decided to go into the pain and hold it as not being just about my partner, but about me and how painful it was to feel rejected. The feelings felt like a black hole and letting them exist rather than fighting against them or rectifying the situation would somehow kill me, as though I were screaming, "NOOOOO!!" inside. I learned I had to go through the black hole to reach the deep, deep Love. I had to let go of my commitment to the idea that what had happened was not okay. Ouch! I felt the pain in my heart around letting go of this idea and my desire to protect my "self" from the experience. It led to a stabbing feeling in my heart to which I just continued opening and opening, feeling as though I were going deeper inside it. It was as though I were letting myself fall into a pit that seemed bottomless and was sure to destroy me. Somewhere inside I finally reached the bottom, however. Or maybe what happened was that a part of me was successfully destroyed and what was left was Love.

Either way, the tears ceased and when I began to look around in this new place I had a true sense that everything was okay and nothing had to change on the outside for me to feel Wholeness and Love inside. From that place I could feel compassion for the scared boy inside my partner who made him pull away, and I could continue to love him. My suffering over the idea of being rejected had melted, as I was consumed by God's love for me. Every time a similar scenario happened with my partner it bothered me less and less, but strangely he began to pull away less and less also. One way to understand this change is that if someone acts as though he or she cannot survive without something, the other cannot afford to cooperate with that myth—we do not want someone's life to depend on us. Once I filled the need with the real Source of Caring, then my partner was free to give more. Through Love, a dynamic that has the potential to destroy a relationship can be transformed into one of patient healing for both people.

Projections

I have been focusing mostly on healing through the heart and engaging the feelings and impressions that arise there, but mental awareness can also alleviate pain and indirectly lead to healing. For instance, an awareness may change an outer behavior or dynamic that then leads to receiving more love from your partner, which touches and mends the deeper issues. One key awareness in your process of self-healing is to look for projections and how your relationship or a particular dynamic mimics the past. Projecting is when you emotionally make a person into a different person you have known or know in your life, or when you view a present experience heavily through the eyes of past experiences, causing feelings that are more in relation to another person or situation than to the one in front of you. For example, a woman who had a quiet and emotionally unavailable father may feel that other men in her life are that way when they are not. Or, when faced with a shy man, the woman may feel unloved, desperate, anxious, or any other feelings she felt when she was with her father, even if the man loves her very much.

Insight into how we make people in our lives into people from our past is central in undoing this tendency. When you begin to understand that your wife's behavior particularly bothers you because you believe it means something it meant when you were with your mother, it helps in reality-testing whether or not that interpretation is also true in the present. Most people want to deny projection is happening because the projection feels so real. If true projection is at work, then you will be absolutely convinced you are right about your perceptions. It takes time, insight, and staying open to new information to slowly learn to see with the eyes of God rather than the eyes of our injuries and past experiences.

It proves helpful to have a sense of humor about these things. We are all irrational at times, so it is nothing about which to be ashamed. Clients often ask me if I think they are crazy, and I am always tempted to say: "Of course!! Aren't we all?" In fact, you are way ahead of the average person if you are even considering that your perceptions are not the reality, that you may be projecting your past onto your present, or one relationship onto another. I am particularly sensitive, for instance, to my husband's attempts to influence how I cook or do a project, etc, because my father tended to micromanage activities occurring around him. When I feel myself digging in my heels and resisting my husband's assistance with how I am doing something, I can smile to myself and realize that I am rebelling against my father in that moment. We do not have to be perfect people (we can't, and if we try we'll be miserable!), we just have to have humility, mercy for ourselves, and a sense of humor.

Humor & Mercy

I think God has a sense of humor too! One of my friends was working on healing a painful feeling and he was asking God what to do next in exploring and healing this experience. Somehow he repeatedly felt moved to yell "Ooga Booga!" He ignored this impulse several times and continued to ask God what to do next, because he could not believe he was supposed to yell "Ooga Booga," especially in a crowded workshop of people practicing healing together. After the third or fourth time in which he was clearly moved to yell "Ooga Booga," and since nothing else was happening in the healing, he felt stuck. He finally decided to trust what he had received in guidance and yelled as loud as he could, "Ooga Booga! Ooga Booga!" As soon as he did this, he began to sob because he could feel the gorilla inside him and was able to move into and slowly heal a large piece of anger he had not been able to access. I always remember "Ooga

Booga!" when I start to take myself too seriously. Life and healing can be creative, surprising, humorous, and fun!

As we all know, part of lightening up is seeing the big picture, yet we forget to do this. If we were better able to laugh at ourselves we would be more open to seeing the bigger picture and realizing how small some of our irritants are. We would be better able to laugh at ourselves if we had more mercy for ourselves, so we have come full circle to opening to receiving God's qualities and holding ourselves and our experiences in those qualities. Humans tend to create such high stakes for things and believe in those stakes. For instance: "If I do not stop eating sugar I will look ugly and be unhealthy and no one will like me." Then, when people naturally are tempted to eat sugar and do so, they feel awful about it and so stressed that they have to eat more sugar to cope!

So, holding ourselves, our choices, and our experiences with more mercy does not only apply to our relationships. In fact, most of the teachings in this chapter can be applied to all areas of life. Children, for instance, are able to change bad habits much more rapidly through a parent's love, acceptance, and support than through harsh punishment and judgment. Why do we not give ourselves the same mercy? If we are able to laugh and say: "Oops!" and connect with Love and Compassion on this human journey of messing up countless times, we begin to embody the qualities of our Creator, while also making it easier for ourselves to actually heal and change for the better.

HEALING YOURSELF

Involving Your Beloved

To this point we have been talking about the kind of healing you can undertake by yourself, so you are reliant on no one but God. If your beloved or friends are not available for support, you can still walk through your heart's feelings to return to Wholeness. For some deeper issues, however, you may decide at some point in your process that you need more care from the outside. A therapist, friend, or healer can be very helpful in holding Love for these places in you and in providing a safe and healing space for your feelings. As the Beatles put it: "We get by with a little help from our friends."

You also may feel that you need your beloved to know this part of you or love you in this place of pain or anger. When you do bring up your feelings with your beloved, however, do it without blame to the best of your capacity. Check to see if your real motive for talking about this issue with your beloved is to get support in looking at your feelings, or that you still believe the problem is in him/her and you want to tell him/her about it so he/she can change. Many people shoot themselves in the foot by disabling their caregiver right at the moment they are asking for care. For instance, blame will trigger a partner into defense, a position from which it will be difficult for the partner to genuinely connect with your heart and to help you. Instead, come to your beloved from a place of self-responsibility, asking for support in exploring your feelings and looking as a team at what happened. Even if you believe that a large part of the needed change is in your partner, approaching it this way will create the broadest possible healing context for you, while also providing the highest probability that your partner will be open enough to discern his/her role in the pain and shift his/her behavior accordingly.

To take a light example, suppose I am feeling anger and anxiety because I want to decorate our home but my husband does not like anything I suggest. Rather than discussing another round of decorating ideas and becoming dismayed when he does not like them or has some reason to put them on hold, then trying to bully him into going along with my plan by expressing how unbearable and frustrating this process is for me, and then becoming even more upset when that does not work, I could first take self-responsibility. So, I would go inside with the pain and feel its different aspects, opening to Love as much as possible, and not hold the belief that my suffering has anything to do with my beloved or his actions, but instead being curious about how such a small outer situation seemed to throw off my connection to Peace and Love. After spending some time with this, I still feel how difficult it is inside and would like to share my struggle with my husband.

I could say: "I am feeling a sense of chaos and anxiety about our decorating process. It is bringing up so much frustration in me to not have things going the way I want. Could you comfort me in this place and help me look at why this is so painful for me?" Hopefully, he is able to stay open to me because he does not feel attacked or blamed for my feelings. Instead, I hope he would feel I needed his help and

HEALING YOURSELF

we could work on something together. I am in a much better position for healing if I am able to receive his love, than if I think my anger and chaotic feeling are about him and therefore close myself to him or, even worse, attack him.

We can explore together the roots of my pain, such as perhaps my father had a chaotic childhood and what he felt was then transmitted to me growing up, such that losing any control brings up fear and anxiety for me. Though this process is focused on me, my husband also gains a deeper compassion for my urgency around what probably had seemed to him a silly issue. His new understanding will help us be a stronger team next time a similar situation arises. Or, perhaps rather than helping me explore why I may feel the way I do to gain insight into my feelings, he just allows me to continue talking about how it feels and he comforts me. Understanding the deeper cause of emotions is usually not necessary for healing, only the Love is ultimately necessary.

Again, though my discussion with my husband may cause him to have more compassion for me and therefore try to work through the issues that prevent him from allowing me to move forward with decorating at my own pace, this outcome cannot be my goal. He will change in who knows how many helpful ways based on our connection, but if he does not I still would know he loves me and would be learning to feel peace no matter how the house looks. I would be on my way to being more robust, holy, peaceful, and happy, no matter what does or does not change around me. Even if my husband is not able to connect with me at all in this place, God can.

If your partner is not skilled enough to be helpful in your healing process even when you come to him/her without blame, then you must take your time and be very gentle and loving with yourself as you work through the issue in your heart on your own in the process described in this chapter. If you get stuck you may need to ask a friend or therapist to sit with you and hold the Love while you feel and process your concerns. Once you have returned to Love inside, you may have some useful feedback for your beloved, but it will come from a desire to help him/her in his/her walking to wholeness, making it easier to receive. You no longer have a stake in things being different. So, if sharing your concerns does not have the desired effect, you still feel okay inside and are able to continue being your beautiful self, which feels great to you and is most likely to call forth your beloved's beautiful self as well.

In conclusion, the process of self healing and returning to Love involves taking self-responsibility, feeling one's feelings fully—unattached to their supposed cause, and relating to those feelings with Love, Compassion, and Mercy, surrendering to what is and staying tuned to see what is next rather than saying "no" to the experience. This practice allows us to use life's events for their intended purpose—the call and response where we can have a relationship with the Divine and learn to drink from the Love that is always available. You can allow yourself to be moved by the One who heals. It is comforting to know you are not the healer because it means you get to relax and receive rather than having to DO anything. You can, however, learn

HEALING YOURSELF

ways to open to the love of the Healer, and remind yourself that you are receiving His care. This process is somewhat similar to that of having your clothes on fire and remembering that you are standing beside a swimming pool. You do not have to put out the fire, you just have to jump into the water! A lot of healing is remembering the Love that is already available to you and drinking from the Source. Through the true Lover, we can all learn to be surrendered to God in whatever life brings us—fully facing and feeling what is.

Chapter Four

Healing Your Beloved

"You must be polite with your beloved and give your whole self to this love. Sometimes God manifests through your beloved as the beauty, and sometimes as the severity. He who cannot accept both is not in the unity, because He is manifesting what He wants you to see of Himself. Give the love to your beloved, and it will change the darkness to the light, the severity to the garden of love. Care for your beloved. Make each word and action contain only the love of God and His politeness. Understand what God wants from you in every minute. What He wants is for you to be the father and the mother, sister and brother, wife and husband to your beloved, to be everything at any time....send mercy to your beloved because in this giving you are sending mercy for yourself.[vii]*"*

Every person has wounds from the past that will be carried into relationships. So, in addition to giving yourself the deep love and mercy around your feelings and seemingly unmet needs, you will need to do the same for your beloved to bring healing to him/her as well. This process is not any easier than looking at one's own issues, but the essence of Compassion from God that you give to yourself and your beloved creates deep and permanent changes that will transform your life profoundly. Remember that if you can give your beloved the real medicine to heal his/her issues even when it requires a high level of patience and steadfastness, you will reap the benefits as much as your partner, both because your development will blossom through the strengthening of your beautiful qualities and because the healing your beloved receives will allow him/her to give you more of what you are wanting.

Beware of the Elicited Response

Love is the healer. Though the love in a relationship can weaken, or even be eclipsed by feelings such as rage if things are difficult over a long period of time, most of us deeply love our partners underneath whatever immediately stronger feelings are distracting us from that or covering it over. So, why aren't our wounds easily healed and bathed in this love? The problem is that our behaviors and feelings elicit a response that will maintain them, rather than heal them. Say a woman is angry about being neglected by her family as a child. As she becomes close to her partner she may show her anger at the slightest hint of his not giving her enough love or not loving her in the way she wants. When she acts out her anger, her beloved's natural response is to pull away, thereby giving her even less of the love she desires. This withdrawal of love seems to prove her initial fears of not being loved and increases her anger, beginning a vicious cycle that maintains her anger and his withdrawal.

HEALING YOUR BELOVED

In this example both the underlying feeling (of not having real love) and the behavior (acting out of anger) are perpetuated rather than healed. The man may truly love this woman, but unfortunately this wounded place in her does not receive the love because when that aspect of her surfaces it elicits an unsatisfying response from him. This process prevents the love in him from reaching the places inside her that need it. The key moment for healing is when the issue shows itself—opening itself to receive. So, the very moment we are triggered by our partner's issue is the moment that healing of the issue can occur if we do not act in the way the issue reflexively stimulates us to respond. For love to reach the places that need it, we have to seize the opportunity and act against our immediate impulse that would reinforce our partner's issue rather than heal it (in our example, withdrawal in the face of anger versus giving the love that is needed to heal the issue because lack of love caused the anger in the first place).

Sometimes just the partner's feeling, not even acted out in obvious ways, will elicit a response that maintains it. For instance, people who feel unattractive often behave in subtle ways that make them much less attractive than those who feel attractive, leading to their being treated as less attractive and reinforcing their picture that this is so. Strong unconscious messages we send to others can cause us to be treated in particular ways. Returning to our earlier example, consciously the woman wants to experience reciprocal love, while unconsciously she wants to elicit what passed for "love" in her childhood. As a child she bonded to the emotional state related to being neglected, so as an adult she is compelled to recreate this state in her relationships. The psychological term for this dynamic is "repetition compulsion." So, we are back to the important point that healing happens when you do <u>not</u> respond in the way your beloved's issue provokes you to respond. You decline the invitation to repeat your beloved's past and instead give your beloved the chance to connect to you in a way that satisfies his or her underlying need.

Giving to your beloved right at the moment when she or he is acting out (the exact moment required to heal it) takes more conscious effort and true patience than you might anticipate. Remember that you would be overcoming a powerful natural survival response that would otherwise take whatever form you developed as a child to protect yourself. The inner struggle we meet at that moment is perfect because it requires us to receive Divine help and ultimately to heal our own issues as well. The saying: "Anything of value takes effort" is certainly true in healing. When you decide you want to make the effort to bring real healing to your beloved, you will need to turn to God with sincerity for help with at least three things: (1) overcoming your own reaction so that you can give what is needed to heal the issue rather than maintain it, (2) discerning the true medicine for your partner's heart in this issue (it may not be as obvious as "love" was in the example we used!), and (3) delivering this medicine to your beloved. The medicine must come from your deepest heart where God gives to you and moves you to give. Let's look at each of these steps that will be necessary in healing your beloved, your child, or anyone else in your life who needs it.

Containment & Remembrance

So, first you must be able to contain your own emotional reaction to your partner's behavior or emotion without responding in the way it elicits. The word "contain" appears fitting, because you are likely to have a reaction (if you didn't, no problem would exist) and you are simply trying to manage that reaction inside you without acting it out, similar to containing a fire. A container is a holding space, as a bowl or pitcher contains water so that it does not spill out everywhere. When we contain, we lovingly hold and make space for something, in contrast to "holding in." It is vital not to "swallow" or suppress the feeling you are having because doing so can lead to exploding later, depression, or sometimes to physical disease. Instead, we must make room inside to experience the feelings fully, but not act them out or act them in. Acting out is taking your feelings out on others (acting from your emotion), while acting in is when you direct your hurt or anger at yourself (such as through self-criticism). The alternative to these, containment, increases with practice, but here are some ideas for beginning this process.

First, the most effective way to contain something is to heal it. If you have time, take your emotional reaction into the process for healing yourself described in the previous chapter. Otherwise, you must engage in a modified version of the same thing—quickly feeling your feelings and physical sensations, and doing remembrance. Remembrance is the process of remembering God. The Divine is always available for help, but we forget He's present with us. Your hurt or angry reaction to your beloved is a cue—a reminder—to turn to God for assistance. Then, begin repeating the name of God to yourself from your heart over and over. You can engage in this practice silently while continuing a conversation or activity with your partner. Repeating the name of God reminds your heart moment to moment that God sustains you and is giving you what you need with each breath. Really soaking this information in will greatly help you contain your reaction. Remembrance also invokes the presence of God, as you are *calling* upon Him.

For this latter part, it is helpful to use a name for God that is truly holy. The science of sounds has determined that in some languages the sound of a word is closely linked to what the word means—you might guess what the word means by hearing it. Sacred languages invoke the presence of the thing named. English, unfortunately, does not. The more ancient languages, such as Aramaic, Sanskrit, Hebrew, and Arabic, do. For instance, saying the word "God" may not create a very holy feeling inside (you can try it now and see what you think), but the words for God in the sacred languages appear more able to provide this experience. For instance, Jesus spoke Aramaic. So, his word for God was "Allaha." Similarly, Christians, Jews, and Muslims in Arabic-speaking countries all refer to God as "Allah."

Various Hebrew terms for the Divine are used in the Old Testament of the Christian bible, or the Jewish Torah, such as "Eloheim," or "Adonai." Jesus also called God "Abba," meaning "daddy," reflecting the tender intimacy of the Divine Love. Hindus or Buddhists may use the Sanskrit word "Om." You may choose the name for God that feels right to you and draw out the sound in a way that resonates in your body and suggests to you the majesty of the One you are inviting to be with you.

To summarize, when your beloved is in an issue that needs healing and is acting in a way that brings up a painful reaction in you, try to contain your reaction by immediately beginning remembrance in your heart while feeling your feelings and bringing them to the name of God you are softly or silently repeating. Let the name take over and feel the aliveness of the Divine moving through you. You are remembering that you have another choice than your initial reaction—you have Love. When you act, you will act from your deep heart, which is more patient and compassionate, not from the issue that was stirred up and would maintain your partner's issue. If you can pause at the critical moment you can break free from automatic responses and receive deeper inspiration by allowing yourself to be held by God. To increase your containment it can also help to connect with your partner's deeper heart, rather than the outer part that is triggering you. Go behind what he or she is showing you on the outside to the deep qualities that attracted you to him or her in the first place. Or, look at the issue that has surfaced as your partner's vulnerability, even if it feels toxic or scary to you. You are emotionally safe if you stay connected to Love, which will be easier if you see the pain that is causing your partner's behavior. Sometimes it helps containment to picture your beloved at age 3, or 5, or 10, innocently struggling to manage the environment that led to this issue forming.

Your containing your reaction without acting it out will be healing for your beloved in itself because his/her issue is so accustomed to being met with the hurtful response it stimulates in others. So, even if it takes everything you have to contain your reaction, you have given your beloved a deep gift that over time will be transformative. If you are able to, however, you may take the next step, which is to give the exact medicine that the issue needs for healing most quickly. Many times an issue will be present for days or weeks, so you may have many opportunities to give the medicine. In most cases it seems we have time to sit and consider what could heal this part of him or her—what our partner's heart needs in this wounded place from which he or she is acting. Even if a heated moment occurs in which you cannot bring yourself to give, containment with no reaction allows you time to think and later come back with the healing response.

Identifying the Medicine

So, how do you discover the needs of your beloved's deep heart? As you read on you might want to choose one of your partner's issues so that you can have it in mind and practice as we explore this process. First, feel what your beloved is like when this issue displays itself. You may close your eyes and really sense the quality of his or her being. Then look a little deeper and open to sense the pain underneath. What is it saying? Some examples might be: "There is never enough," "Life is unfair to me," "No one cares about me," "If I love, I get hurt," "I'm unworthy," "I'm out of control," "I do everything and have no support," "I can't trust people," "Things are going to fall apart," etc.

As you connect with the pain, feel that for which it is longing. If you can speak right to this place in your beloved's heart, true healing will occur. Perhaps a sense of stability is needed, or mercy, or freedom, or understanding, or patience, or respect. Many healing qualities exist and you want to choose the exact aspect of Love that will give most deeply to your partner's need. As you sense the place in your beloved that is crying, from your heart ask God what will heal this place and then listen quietly inside for the answer. You may receive direct knowing, or see an image, or hear a voice, or feel the quality that is needed pouring over you. Sink into the place in you that loves your partner and swim in that. From that place open to the flow of Divine guidance. Relax and open to receive.

Your guidance for what the medicine is may surprise you or may not make logical sense, but as long as it comes with a subtle sense of gentle peace, light, or love when you think of it, you are on the right track and should trust what you get. An example where the solution was not obvious, was when a friend's family moved and was sharing a house with another family. My friend's daughter began biting people regularly, which she had never done before. My friend went through the process described to discern what was amiss for his daughter. He saw that behind the biting was her feeling confused about boundaries and how to live in this new home (this connection was not readily apparent on the outside, but when he felt her heart he could see it). She needed clarity and holding. He picked up his daughter and walked her through the whole house, explaining as they went along what were her toys and where she was allowed to play and what each space was for, etc., really trying to help her understand their new home and how she was to be in it so that she could feel safe. After that she never bit anyone again! As you can see, it is much more effective to give the real medicine than it is to try to fix the symptom (in this example, telling this little girl not to bite or punishing her for doing so).

Delivering the Medicine

Receiving from God remains paramount as you transition from perceiving what the medicine is for your beloved as discussed, to the last step of healing your beloved—actually delivering the medicine to your beloved's heart. The deeper your connection with the Divine, the more powerful and effective your delivery of the medicine. Whatever flavor of love this wound needs is a flavor on which God is an expert. You can ask for that quality to come directly from Him, through you, to your beloved's deep heart. So, ideally you are merely a conduit through which Divine qualities can be transmitted to you partner.

HEALING YOUR BELOVED

To do so, you must be able to receive from God—to fill up with the quality you want to give and to let it move through you. If you intuit, for instance, that your partner does not feel safe, then take a few minutes to feel safe in your own heart. Let the deep understanding of safety come to you from God. When you have opened to receive something beautiful, allow it to become your reality, filling you completely until it simply spills over to your partner. It is as though your heart is teaching your beloved's heart to feel safe by showing it the experience: "Oh, my beloved, taste this!" Though it may be true that you have to give to receive, it is certainly true in this case that you have to receive to give.

Then, you must also connect all the way (or as deeply as you can) with the place that is hurting in your partner. Do not leave that place alone or rejected anymore. Help it receive what it needs by delivering right to the spot. Many people shy away from pain, or ugly parts, in ourselves and others. Though it is not always fun to connect with them, these are the parts that are crying and truly need us to move toward, rather than away, from them. If you feel scared as you try to connect, or perhaps it feels too intimate, then you have found another part of you that could receive more. Perhaps you need strength or trust, or more of a sense that it is not you connecting to the pain, but that you are simply sending a transmission from the Source of Love. In any case, take time to notice what surfaces in you in the process of receiving from the Divine and in connecting fully with the places of pain in your beloved. Take any difficulties in these processes into remembrance and the self-healing methods previously described.

Sometimes issues are ripe and are just begging to have a healing response so they can clear. You can feel people who put out something that would naturally elicit a negative reaction, but behind what they display on the outside they are praying and hoping for someone to love them anyway and give what is needed to lift the burden of the painful reality in which they are trapped. These issues can move quickly when you shift how you are responding to them, and both you and your beloved will feel an immediate deep sense of relief. Other issues are not ready to change so quickly. It may take perseverance on your part, and your beloved may continue to flail inside and act out because it takes time to trust what you are giving and absorb it, or begin to let it soothe the part that needs it.

The hurt place can become scared when it actually receives that for which it was longing. It knows that if it takes in this quality it will have to die (The injured place would have to heal and therefore will no longer exist.). Many times these hurtful defenses that stand to die have saved us from great danger throughout life. Clinging to the pain ensures we remember to protect ourselves from the same thing happening again (hence all the behaviors that stimulate its maintenance). In other words, the issue does not necessarily want to heal, so your beloved may try even more strenuously to trigger the response that maintains it.

A woman who has always lived with yelling fights in her home, for instance, may become increasingly angry if she cannot stimulate her partner to yell at her because of the repetition compulsion described earlier. If the partner can contain her unconscious attempts to elicit this response, she may become initially more panicky and try harder. This reaction occurs partly because she does not know any other way to connect around her pain, so she has learned this way of receiving attention and knowing she is loved (It was how she connected with her family growing up!). To some degree, her whole way of seeing the world will collapse if she cannot provoke someone into fighting with her, especially someone she deeply loves. So, healing this repetition compulsion can be scary and may be rejected for some time because the self would have to rearrange so drastically if the issue disappeared. In this case when you give to your beloved, the behavior or issue may temporarily worsen, but if you are gentle and persistent your partner will learn a new way to love and be able to receive the deep gifts you are offering.

Another factor in how long the healing process can take is the level to which you have really surrendered to God and are truly experiencing the quality you are giving. If you are sending a little compassion, but are also furious and therefore mixing in anger and resentment, you partner will be smart not to absorb much. I have found sometimes I will be trying on the outside to give what is needed, but inside I utterly reject or hate the part of my beloved I am trying to heal. Of course I cannot expect my husband to come running into my arms if (metaphorically speaking, of course) I have a knife hidden behind my back! In contrast, I have found that when

I am truly with the Divine, my husband recognizes that and accepts whatever comes to him from that place, even if it is scary or difficult for him. It is as though his being bows to my heart, as mine does to his when he is holding Divine Truth.

It can be intimidating to think, however, that you have to be completely immersed in the healing qualities and free of your reactions to give the healing to your beloved. First, I believe our best effort is always good enough. God seems to honor our sincerity and help us when we struggle. If God doesn't change your mixed transmission into a pure one when you are really seeking to serve Him and your beloved, it may be because He wants you to spend more time receiving healing from Him yourself and does not want you to lose the chance to gain the gift of purifying whatever is surfacing in you. Many times, however, He will simply take over and provide a miracle when you are valiantly trying and have surrendered to Him.

For instance, returning to the past partner I mentioned earlier who was scared of intimacy, many times when I reached out he would pull away. One time we were intimately relating and he suddenly turned away and began ignoring me, even when I attempted to touch him or talk to him. I felt my heart aching so deeply it felt as though a huge pulsing weight were in my chest, almost as though my heart were going to break. I was hurt, but also angry as a reaction to my hurt, and I wanted to run out of the room and never speak to him again. I withdrew and paused to feel my pain and decide what to do. I decided to open to some compassion by considering what issue might be triggered in him that was causing this behavior. I immediately saw that he was terrified of abandonment because of his childhood experiences and so when he began to get close to me he felt petrified and immobilized. The only thing he could bring himself to do in that regressed place was to turn away.

I asked God what he needed to heal this place, and the answer I felt was that he needed to know I was there and not going anywhere, even when he was scared and acting out as he was in that moment. You can see how my gut reaction to the situation, which was to leave him, would have maintained or worsened his issue by proving it was correct—that he would, indeed, be abandoned and could not trust I would be there for him. As I considered these things I knew I needed to communicate to him the medicine I had discovered, but inside I did not feel the desire to do so. I continued to feel an enormous sinking in my chest and everything in me still wanted to leave the relationship that moment and never look back.

I told God that I would try to give, but that I did not feel it was true--that I really loved him or was there for him--and I really needed Him to speak for me. It took everything I had to turn back toward my partner. When I opened my mouth to speak, however, the entire weight and pain that I had felt so powerfully inside lifted in an instant and I felt free and light. As the words of love came out of my mouth, they were completely heart-felt and true, even moving me to tears with the rich caring and patience I felt. My partner turned back around with his heart more open than I had ever experienced it. He began interacting with me so sweetly and intimately. Looking back I appreciate the courage it took to give something different than what his behavior elicited and how God responded by healing me (instantaneously!) as well and allowing me to give something that I could not have given on my own.

That profound fear my partner had at the time was significantly healed in that moment and never resurfaced to the same degree, even though it was the kind of deep issue that could hurt a marriage for 30 years or more and still not change. So, give your best shot and God will support you and give you exactly what you need. Overcoming your gut reaction and doing something holy instead is more than just beautiful, it is the seed of world peace. If we can do it in our relationships, we can do it in our communities, and in our country, and in our relationship with other countries and peoples. To have love between people we have to choose the Divine instead of our triggered reactions. Let your heart be a place that demonstrates Love defeating hate, even when the battle is difficult and your "self" might be a casualty.

Ultimately, patience is key. It will help to keep the long run in mind and to support your beloved in becoming his or her highest self. My husband is great at this piece. Sometimes I will discover that I had been doing something that he did not like, and ask him why he had not told me. Several times his answer has been something like: "Well, just because I do not like it today doesn't mean I won't like it in the future. I get the sense that if you changed this behavior to accommodate my preference it would not actually help you in becoming a better person. I would hate to ask you to change something based on my present reactions and then 10 years from now wish you were the way you were before!" We do not want our partners to change to make our issues more comfortable. It would be better to have our issues stimulated so that we can see them clearly and heal them. Even when it is an issue of your beloved's that needs healing for his or her spiritual growth and personal development, if you continue to keep an eye on the long-run you can appreciate the tiny changes and give space for your beloved's unfolding. He or she does not need to be the perfect person today. The growth process is the meat of life, not something to get over with!

Meeting the Feeling

A central aspect of healing, which goes along with the process previously described, is being with and respecting your beloved's feelings. A basic desire of every person is to be known. When your beloved is having a strong feeling or reaction, it is healing if you can deeply listen and acknowledge his or her pain. Men, in particular, often want to solve a problem if they are faced with one, and therefore become overwhelmed and feel inadequate when their partners are presenting an unsolvable or irrational conflict or issue. If they can learn the power of just listening and caring, they can feel more effective in meeting their beloved's needs and therefore less overwhelmed, enabling them to stay with, and contain, their beloveds' feelings or problems with more stamina than when they felt responsible for fixing something.

People seem to have the greatest struggle listening to and understanding their partner's feelings when they disagree with the causes for the feelings. For instance, if your beloved described a scenario in which he or she was clearly at fault, but is concluding that he or she was mistreated and is distraught about it, you may have the impulse to point out the other person's perspective or discount your beloved's feelings as being silly or wrong. This tendency is even greater if you just happen to be the person that created your partner's anger or hurt. The important thing to understand in these situations is that you can support your partner and care for his or her feelings without agreeing with their supposed cause. The content of *why* he or she is having those feelings is mostly irrelevant compared with the importance of the simple fact that you care that he or she is suffering.

I remember one time when I was very angry and exasperated with my husband and we were in a deadlock about whether or not what he was doing was okay. It felt so important to me that he say he was wrong and do what I wanted that I became distraught when he would not budge on his opinion. He put his arm around me as I was crying and said he was there for me and that I could just keep feeling the feelings and he would hold me. At first I wanted to lash out and say it could not be okay if he did not see that he had been hurtful and wrong, so I said something about how he needed to apologize. He simply said, in a loving tone, that he continued to disagree with me about the content of what happened (he did not think he did anything wrong), but that he was fully here for me to explore what it brought up in me. As he continued to make supportive space for me to feel my feelings, I began to melt. I really felt my being relax and become quiet. I became aware that not feeling loved had caused the original conflict and that in this moment he was giving me love and really feeding my heart. The issue of who was right or wrong did not matter and so I let it go. This encounter illustrates how addressing the content of what caused the feelings and caring for the feelings themselves are two completely separate processes. They far too often become intertwined in a way that prevents giving each other the love we need around our raw emotions. I could feel at the time how my husband was bowing to my heart, which is really bowing to God in me. The Divine lives within each of us—it's the essence of our creation. So, when you surrender to your beloved, surrender to the deepest part of him or her that knows Love and that holds the beauty of the spirit. Seeing the face of God in your beloved is a helpful way to increase your containment and patience.

Being the Earth

A very holy station (place in spiritual development) is achieved when you can "be the earth" for someone. The earth allows us to walk on her and supports us always, without asking for anything in return. God takes care of her and gives her the rain and all her other needs to carry out her purpose. Most of us cannot hold this station for very long without resentment because we are not fully in the station, but merely trying to be. Still, visiting and tasting this station before we are able to live there helps us prepare for and realize this potential. When truly embodying this station there is no sense of being a victim, only the bounty of Divine support and the beauty, majesty, and freedom in real selflessness. ==When you are really the earth for people in the sincere and humble way with God's support, ironically you are irresistible and everyone wants to be near you, love you, and respect you.==

To conclude, healing is as simple as opening your heart and letting God's qualities pour through you to your beloved's heart. No words are necessary to heal at this deep level, though sometimes when you see what is needed to heal the place of pain you can deliver right to that place the perfect words to address the concern. Simply serve your beloved by offering what he or she needs. If you want to give the medicine, but you find your heart is full of anger or hurt instead, try not to judge yourself or create more separation, but know that this is your chance to heal yourself as well. You need to receive the Divine qualities and mercy as much as anyone. Hold yourself in love and care for the places in you that need healing and then you will be able to give the real remedy for what is aching in your beloved's heart. We are all held in God's Love and Compassion. I pray we can all lift the veils to witness this reality and live from there, so we, our families, and our communities will drink deeply from this ocean.

Chapter Five

Healing Your Relationship

"When the fire of his love touches the essence of the love of the soul of the woman he loves, then the sparks and the waves of flame flash out and return to their source in the blaze of divine passion, and his body disappears, and her body also disappears. All the veils, all the fascination of coming and going between them disappears in the experience of their indivisible unity, and God returns to love Himself alone. But he created these people and the fire between them to realize the essence of His love. Whereas, in the beginning, the man thought he loved a woman, when he comes to realize the essence of the fire, he sees that he himself is the Beloved and she is also the Beloved and in this, God is the Beloved and no other exists[xii]."

When you heal yourself or your beloved, as discussed, you are also healing your relationship. Your relationship constitutes a third entity with its own level of well-being. When the relationship is healthy, the individuals in the relationship can bring their problems to this third party and receive help and support even when a problem has to do with the other person in the relationship. For instance, if I feel the house is too messy when I get home from work, rather than blame my husband for this, I bring the problem to the relationship to solve. I might say to my beloved that I feel anxious when I arrive home and the tables are covered with things. He may say, "Hmm…I feel trapped when everything has to look that neat—as though I were living in a museum." Now we have a problem for the relationship to solve. The relationship cares about each person's feelings and will have to invent a solution that best meets the needs of its members. In other words, we both care about each other's feelings, so we can take the information from both sides and work together on a solution. We are playing on the same team! Neither of us must create a solution by ourselves, nor are we acting as adversaries.

Teamwork & Goodwill

Developing this sense that you are on the same team with your beloved, rather than each side battling its position, proves vital in resolving conflict and protecting the health of the relationship. If you do not feel you function as a team, continue envisioning how that would look and move in that direction. You could start by finding a place where you and your beloved *are* on the same team. Perhaps when it comes to parenting, having fun outings together, your business partnership (making financial decisions, etc), or some other aspect of the relationship, the relationship functions as a trust-worthy third party that is stronger, more fun, and smarter than either individual. If these areas are not apparent at first, look deeper to where they are. Perhaps you share some core values with your beloved and this connection really strengthens and feeds both of you at that level.

Playing on the same team requires having goodwill toward your partner. "Where there's goodwill there's a way!" Without goodwill, healing the relationship may be impossible, because this key ingredient is the sustenance for relationships—creating stability and trust in difficult times and always nurturing the love. If goodwill toward each other has faded, what is needed to rebuild it? The healing methods described previously are important in addressing the pain that is likely to exist behind each person's lack of goodwill toward the other, but now rather than looking at the heart of each person, we are addressing the heart of the relationship. Attributions play an important role.

Attributions

Attributions are powerful beliefs we hold about particular things or people. We attribute to them certain qualities or motives and see them in this light. These develop over time in relationships and, when negative, quickly erode goodwill. You may have the attribution, for instance, that your partner is irresponsible. So, when he or she forgets to pick up the kids or leaves the oven on, it reaffirms your attribution and leads to any number of negative feelings about the relationship. If, instead, you think your beloved IS responsible, then these mistakes are viewed merely as human error and are not as painful. Even if the errors cause you trouble or hurt your feelings, they do not hurt the relationship because they do not cause a negative view of your beloved and the relationship, which would diminish good will.

Once we have negative attributions, we are likely only to see evidence that supports our attributions and to ignore the conflicting evidence. This dynamic makes it difficult for our partners to change in our eyes, and even to change in reality, because we elicit the behavior we expect. It is very difficult, for instance, to act like an adult when your partner treats you like a child. Unfortunately, people are also primed for making particular attributions representing aspects of life that they had to be particularly aware of as children. Thus, someone who learned growing up that it is very dangerous to be with someone untrustworthy, might attribute untrustworthiness to his or her partner after the commission of one or two mistakes anyone might make. In other words, we are psychologically primed for false positives in particular areas, which happen to be our most painful areas and the ones most likely to threaten our goodwill toward our partner, or our experience of goodwill from him or her.

If you have the attribution that your partner is critical, then you are likely to perceive his or her facial expression as critical even when it is actually neutral. Just to experiment with attributions and their effects on your relationship, in your next neutral conversation with your beloved, assume he or she is feeling deeply in love with you and is thinking inside how amazing you are. See how the conversation feels. Then you can try assuming he or she is hating you inside and see how different your experience is (don't do this one for very long!). As you can see, negative attributions will constantly undermine the health of a relationship.

Couple's therapy is a very productive way to address negative attributions, and the pain they cause you and your partner, because your therapist will notice behaviors or assumptions of which you might not be aware. To address those attributions of which you are conscious, however, simply try not to make generalizations about your beloved and begin noticing exceptions and counter-evidence. You will have to put on your detective hat and really notice little things that go against your belief so that you can build a case against your attribution and see things more realistically.

Being Right or in Relationship

One of the most important keys to healing a relationship is handling conflict effectively. You may have heard the saying: "You can either be right or be in relationship." I repeat this saying to myself sometimes when my drive to be right is stimulated. Though I'm not wanting to be right for its own sake, I'm still wanting to be right--perhaps what we are disagreeing about feels important, and so I think my opinion must prevail or some negative consequence will happen! These are the times to remember you are choosing between "right" and "relationship." Why is this choice so difficult? Of course we want love. Who cares about being right? Perhaps being wrong negatively impacts our self-esteem, though it need not be that way. Also, unconsciously we may link another person's being right and our being wrong to their having power over us. This feeling that you are in their hands because you were wrong can stimulate fear of helplessness and being consumed (i.e. losing yourself and dying!)[vi]. Recognizing the irrationality of these strong emotional reasons to be right can help us let go. If any feeling is involved in the conflict, proving your point should be put aside for a time and addressing the emotions in a loving way should become the focus. Logistics can be discussed later so that the precious opportunity to care for feelings is not missed.

Facts vs. Feelings

So, the feelings attached to an issue and the actual issue itself should be discussed separately as much as possible. For instance, if you and your spouse strongly disagree about what school the children will attend next year, the pros and cons of the schools should be one discussion and the anger and other emotional pieces that are involved in disagreeing should be another. For the outer situation it may help to pretend you are talking about a neighbor's problem, not yours, in order to maintain some level of emotional detachment and to consider the facts from as neutral a position as possible. The separate conversation about feelings, apart from the problem-solving conversation, should take precedence. A moment of feeling is a chance for healing and to know each other more deeply. If one of you is triggered into the past (present pain is frequently brought up because of past experiences, often childhood), you do not want to waste the chance to understand what is operating in the relationship and look at it together. If you can make space inside yourself for people to feel whatever they are feeling, giving them permission to feel by holding it as okay with you and not something you will take personally, you create space for them to explore it and deepen their experience and understanding.

To take another example, you may be arguing with your beloved about who contributes more work to the household. Communicating your point of view might seem important because it could affect how much work you will have to do in the future. What actually creates positive change, however, is connection and healing. So, instead of being right, you may choose relationship and help your beloved explore his or her feelings around this topic. You might say: "So, you feel unsupported?" Then allow your partner to vent about this experience for awhile and encourage deepening with a statement such as: "Gosh, I'm really sorry. That sounds so difficult, as though you are working and working and not feeling appreciated or supported. I know that feeling and it is awful!" Then, as he or she feels held in love, your beloved can explore his or her feelings more gently and fluidly, and when it seems to be concluding, you could say: "Is there anything I could do that would help you feel more appreciated for all that you do, or that would help to make it seem less burdensome?"

Giving and receiving emotional support in a conflict is much easier if you each speak in terms of what you are feeling, rather than stating supposed facts. Most "factual" statements are debatable and will inspire argument and disagreement. People find it difficult not to rebut a questionable accusation or a misperception when they hear one. Instead, make your statements about your feelings. No one can argue with how you feel because you are the expert on that, and the only one who knows what is going on inside of you. "You promised you would be on time from now on, and this is the third time you have kept me waiting this week! You don't care about anyone but yourself," are three debatable, and hurtful, statements ready to be argued. Instead, try: "I felt so hurt and disappointed when you arrived late. I had the thought that you don't care about me, and that made me really sad."

Also, when you each state your feelings, there is more on which to agree. If each of you say you feel hurt, for instance, you have already found common ground! You understand each other because you are both feeling the same way and can come together around that and feel empathy and connection, rather than being with the facts, on which you may have very different perceptions and perspectives[xiii].

The Power of Roles

Another method for dealing with conflict in a way that

HEALING YOUR RELATIONSHIP

will heal the relationship rather than hurt it, is to take turns talking rather than both trying to convey your points at once. If one of you speaks and then the other refutes, and so on, no real communication occurs because both people are on the defensive and not taking in anything. What's more, both people are probably thinking of their responses while the other person is speaking, making it difficult to hear any important information that is being voiced. If your beloved is willing to agree that you both will have a chance to speak, and to respond to the other person, but not until the first person has said everything he or she wants to say and the other person has really understood the gems in it, you have created a system which makes containment easier so real growth and learning in the relationship can occur.

Knowing your role, similar to a role in a play, is helpful in relationships. In the scenario just discussed, one person is in the listener role and the other is in the communicator role. The listener's job is to try to understand, rather than trying to be understood, which is often people's goal in a conflict. It is easy to see how stagnation and pain can develop if both people's goal is to be understood and no one's goal is to understand. So, in the listener role, you must not be thinking of a rebuttal inside, but instead really sending your being out to meet your beloved's heart with curiosity and desire to find out what it is he or she feels is so important for you to understand. Your job in this role is to truly hear your beloved.

The speaker's role is to communicate the important information in a way that is most likely to be heard and understood by the other person. The speaker's job is much easier when the other person is in the listener role because an opening exists in the other. For this reason, the speaker is likely to be much more gentle, soft, and calm than he or she would have been otherwise. Aggression is not necessary if you do not have to break through the insurmountable barrier that exists when the two people are refusing to hear each other. In other words, the door is open so no need exists for pounding on the door. Also, actually listening to someone is a loving action, so if the listener is doing his or her role, the speaker's heart will be drinking from the experience of being loved. Some of the hurt, anger, or fear is likely to be dissolving already.

Before switching roles the listener should attempt to repeat what he or she heard to the speaker and see if he or she took in what the speaker was communicating. If the listener has missed the point, then you are not ready to switch roles. Continue with the process until the mail is delivered! Sometimes we are tossing letters toward our beloveds and they are not opening them. The letters are just piling up. Likewise, they are tossing letters at us and we are not opening them either. Pretty soon couples have such a large stack of mail piled up between them that they cannot see each other anymore—they are each just staring at their side of the large, confusing pile of unopened letters. Both people need to stop writing and start reading.

Another way to use roles in managing conflict is to not let both people play the "crazy" role at once. We can lovingly use the term "crazy" for when we go into our issues

HEALING YOUR RELATIONSHIP

and are emotionally triggered because we are most likely out of touch with reality and almost certainly out of touch with our higher selves, most productive coping strategies, and best communication skills. When we are enmeshed in our issues, we have been hijacked into a regressed state in which we do not know how to make the best decisions or to act effectively to build love in our lives. It is vital in relationships that both people do not go crazy at once.

So, if you find that your beloved is crazier than you in any particular issue or moment, it is in the relationship's best interest to switch roles from triggered partner to a helping role. Often both people go crazy at once because one person's craziness stimulates the other person's. Roles play a powerful part in preventing this dynamic. If you truly put aside your role as partner and know your job is to deal in a healing way with this crazy person before you, then you might be able to respond more productively and not become as triggered yourself. Do not try to respond rationally to the irrational. Solving the outer issue will not work in a crazy moment. You must speak lovingly to the little child inside your beloved who is hurt and needing love, or some version of love—patience, holding, containment, reassurance, boundaries, kindness, respect, attention, soothing…. Switching into the role of a good parent, for instance, you can imagine you are the caring, nurturing mother for this beloved before you whose heart is clearly deeply needing something. If you can be in this role with your crazy beloved, you give permission for him or her to really experience the craziness and receive healing in that place.

Now, from a state of craziness your beloved might say something so strong that it transports you out of your loving role and into your craziness, making you even more crazy in that moment than your beloved. Ideally, both people will monitor who is the more crazy at each moment in order to understand their role. If your beloved sees: "Uh-oh, he/she just became more crazy than I am!" then he or she must put aside his or her craziness and switch into a containing role for you. These roles might switch many times during an argument, but to the extent either person is able to hold the healer role with the other, deep appreciation, safety, and love will develop. To reiterate: only one person can be crazy at once. Know your role at any given moment!

Some people have a partner who is not yet capable of engaging in these kinds of practices. It is sad, and much more difficult, to face healing the relationship without support. Remember, however, that should you take on this challenge, you are engaging in your own spiritual walking and are ultimately doing so for the sake of your own development, not just for the sake of the relationship. Always attend to what God is asking from you by listening deep in your heart to what the voice of Love says. Often you'll see how you are being asked to practice the spiritual containment, generosity, and healing that we have been exploring, but sometimes Love may guide you to protect yourself with boundaries or to withdraw from the situation, or even from the relationship.

If you find yourself in a situation in which you are the crazier, but your beloved does not know how to contain you

HEALING YOUR RELATIONSHIP

and shift out of his or her own issues to support you, then you must find a way to be in a healer role with yourself. Before acting from your issues you can realize: "Hold on! The one feeling this is not the person I want running my life!" So, you can instead remove yourself from the situation and give yourself space to turn inward and state your perspective to yourself and explore how it feels. Then, get a second opinion—God's! You might say to God, "This is the way I see it and that feels ☹, now how do YOU see it?" Then simply sit as deeply in your heart as you can to listen to and feel what moves from the Love. Do not stop until the perspective you receive in your heart feels light and pure. Even if you do not yet believe the viewpoint that came to you, now you have another option that feels light and free and you can continue to sit with it and allow it to instruct you over time.

We are ultimately attempting not to play the unhealthy roles we played in our families of origin or stimulate corresponding roles in others. We discussed projection earlier—where we paste people, beliefs, or feelings from our past onto our present loved ones so that we are actually seeing someone else. Projective identification is when the person onto whom we projected starts to behave in accordance with our projection. In other words, we treat them so strongly as though they are or think a certain way that they identify with that and begin to feel or act as our projection said they would. An argument between lovers is often really two children fighting with their parents. Instead of two people, two self-objects are present. A self-object is an internal image from childhood of some person (object) and the way that person related to you. In other words, both people in an argument are working out a childhood dynamic. The first step in better communication is finding a way to actually see the other person as a person—your beloved. In the movie "Story of Us" the couple is pictured fighting in bed, and both partner's parents are lying in the bed with them. So, the 6 people are actually fighting—two parents in each person's head contributing to the heated fight. The scene is humorous, but sadly so real. ==We need to find a way to peel away the transference onto our beloveds of our parents and other past significant relationships, so we can see the actual person with whom we are in relationship.==

Related to the repetition compulsion described previously, we unconsciously tend to choose lovers who recreate for us on some level how we felt growing up, or what we learned love was. In a sense we walk around with an unconscious puzzle piece and feel attraction when another person's unconscious puzzle piece fits into ours. With projective identification, however, even if we escape choosing partners who are similar in unconscious dynamics to one of our parents, we are likely to be able to make our partners into these significant people from the past at some point in the relationship, either in how we view them, or in what behaviors we elicit from them. If we played a role in our family of origin (i.e. caretaker, scapegoat, hero, etc), we are likely to try to play that role in our present family. That role strongly pulls for a corresponding role from your beloved.

HEALING YOUR RELATIONSHIP

For instance, imagine someone speaking to you condescendingly. You are likely to do whatever you did growing up to cope with such a situation—perhaps you became rebellious and tried to start a fight, or perhaps you felt inferior and suddenly could not think straight or perform well. See how one role triggers another? When both people are caught in a role that holds the other person in a corresponding role, the couple must recognize that they are in a role lock[xiv] and that role locks are very powerful. Then, they can take hands and together try to step out of their roles simultaneously, each person being careful not to act out the role that would bring the other person back into his or her role as well.

Good psychotherapy uncovers and disrupts these patterns. In group therapy, where you explore how you relate to others and what feelings arise in relationships, people often relate to other group members in ways directly connected to their childhoods. Clients in my therapy groups often enjoy the joke: "If it's not one thing, it's your mother!" We all have sensitive areas and our partners need to understand what those are, how they came to be, and how difficult and painful they are. If you really know your partner's wounds, it is easier not to take things personally. You can have empathy when the same criticism of you or anxiety in particular kinds of situations surfaces repeatedly. These issues can change, of course, but require patience and healing responses, as discussed.

Biological aspects of a person can become interwoven with roles and make the role much more difficult to change.

For instance, some people do not have a good memory or can't do two things at once, etc. These characteristics can lead to a persona created around these features that interact with corresponding roles from others (one person may have to take the organizing role if the other is absent-minded, for instance). Teasing out nature versus nurture is difficult because they are so intertwined, but it is beneficial to have a general sense about what struggles in your partner are hard-wired so that you can be especially merciful and understanding. If you were not keeping in mind your partner's Attention Deficit Disorder, for instance, you could be hurt by many unintentional behaviors or lack of seeming concentration on you, etc. The ADHD might have allowed your beloved to be hyper-focused on you during dating, but then later something else interesting competes and you feel left. Understanding how ADHD works could allow you not to take this situation personally and to cease imagining that you are not loved. With biological issues, the best goal seems to be awareness, surrender, and acceptance. My husband could more easily tolerate my monthly hurt or crying over small things when he understood PMS (Pre-Menstrual Syndrome) and began to be aware of the role that plays in my sensitivity.

Step by Step

Healing comes to a relationship step by step. Look at your relationship as a whole and feel where the next baby step is. Then you can feel how to support it in making that movement. Just as in healing your partner or yourself, you cannot feed your relationship something it is not able to digest. Parents do not feed meat to infants, but give milk month after month until the infant grows into a person who is able to digest other foods and eventually meat. So, in healing, give what your "baby" relationship can receive.

I remember with one beloved we had a cycle where he would be withdrawn and distant and I knew he needed patience and reliable love to trust me and become more available emotionally. For weeks at a time I would be able to resist complaining about the lack of responsiveness I perceived. I would not demand more from him, though my heart wanted more. These periods were painful for me because I was not in complete containment where I had reached true peace about it, but I was struggling with the issue and trying my best to give what was needed for healing. Though my state was not complete, the healing would work and he would become increasingly open as I worked to appreciate and respond to his good qualities instead of criticizing him for what I was not receiving.

Just as he was giving an amount that would otherwise satisfy me, however, I would feel so overwhelmed from my time of containing him that he would do one little thing that touched that spot and I would give up and dramatically tell him how hurt I was and how he had to change. He would withdraw again in fear of losing me and because he would feel attacked (which was from his father, not me) and I would feel remorse and the cycle would begin again from square one.

The dynamic did not completely change until we were able to move past the breaking point that would send us back repeatedly. To use our earlier analogy, I would feed my beloved milk in this area until he grew strong enough to eat vegetables and other foods, and then suddenly I would get impatient and try to cram meat down his throat, causing him to become sick and regress. The reason I would lose containment was because I was not seeking enough support from the Divine or from other people to really free me of the pain of wanting something I could not yet have.

Holding my goal in mind eventually allowed me to contain him until he was strong enough to take my feedback and not collapse under it. He could then feed me what I needed in return. I was not simply being patient with him and facing my own issues of hurt when I did not feel I was getting enough love (both worthy activities!). I was effectively building something that would forever be different than the present situation. Keeping your eyes on what you believe is needed to create a relationship that will be able to meet your needs deeply and hold your heart, even though it is not capable of doing so at the present time, will give you the strength to weather the difficulties in a way that will lead to a beautiful future.

Intentions & Mistakes

Dogged commitment to your intentions is a basic ingredient for healing a relationship and for spiritual development in general. We are created to mess up over and over again! It is the intentions that navigate our ships and allow us to realize when we have gone off course and steer our way back. We must learn the art of returning because we will always go astray. A spiritual journey is about returning and returning and returning, allowing our powerful commitment to our intentions (and to God) to inspire and guide us. At some point we realize we have not been able to reach our goal, but that should not lead to abandoning our intentions, it should instead be the point where we hold our intentions more fervently than ever and allow God to take over. Those are the moments where true spiritual transformation takes place.

Understanding the beauty of mistakes and being able to be merciful about our (REPEATED!) shortcomings provide the stamina and sustenance to move forward in our spiritual growth. You might lovingly call a state of having gone astray, the "station of the mistake." Spiritual stations are states of development in relationship to God. The word "station" acknowledges that only God is the changer of states, and He has given each of us a station in every moment. When you are in the station of the mistake, look for what the Love is asking you to learn or see. You may have acted from a place of ignorance of God's Truth, so the mistake acts as an arrow pointing you toward a door of deeper knowing. You might blame yourself for whatever decisions you made that led you somewhere less than beautiful inside or outside, but nothing happens without the permission of the Most High. Why did the Source of Beauty bring you to this place? If you remember that the picture you see is only one scene of the show, and do not turn off the movie, but stay with God to let it unfold in His way, you may find the answer to this question. Perhaps you will be led to greater Beauty than you would have reached traveling a route that did not lead through darkness.

Therefore, in relationships we trust Love and surrender to follow It and drink from It to the extent our beings can. We are compassionate about the rest. Much care is needed, however, not to break anything—our heart, our beloved's heart, or the relationship. I once asked my spiritual teacher what to do about conflict in a relationship. He said that the purpose of a cup is to hold milk and honey. He asked me: "Do you throw away the cup when it is empty?" Then he answered: "No!! You will need it again when you have more milk and honey." I believe he was saying that just because the goodies are not flowing in your relationship right now does not mean they will not in the future. Be careful not to break the container of the relationship that you will need to hold those gems when they return.

Connection on Subtle Levels

Taking care of the relationship means doing your best not to hurt your beloved's heart. Hearts are extraordinarily sensitive and subtle. For instance, putting someone down is stealing from them—their dignity and your love. Even if they are not present it seems to affect their hearts. If I joke about my husband to my female friends, he seems different the next time I see him—reserved and a little hurt. Our connections with others are much deeper than the physical, so they transcend time and space. When a couple is deeply committed, they can operate in some ways as one heart and one psyche. Couples, for instance, have unconscious agreements operating beneath the surface all the time. One example is a couple's comfort with a particular level of closeness. If the closeness begins to cross that threshold, the couple will create a fight to regain the proper distance. You and your beloved can understand that because of these unconscious agreements what may look like one person's fault is really an agreed upon action for the sake of the team.

If one person, for instance, returns to an old way of behaving that really hurt the relationship, the other person might say: "Look what WE did!" because he or she knows that the other person's behavior was a way for the team to regain the safety of a comfortable level of separation. Many psychologists would hold that because of unconscious communication, at some level both people in the relationship always know about an extra-marital affair. It is just a matter of at which level of consciousness they allow it to exist.

The subtlety of our impact on each other increases when we consider our spiritual connection with our beloveds, in addition to the psychological. It is sometimes to the point where the two souls are almost one. As a result, a person would know at some level the moment his or her partner began an affair. A friend of mine told me that one night he could not sleep and felt nauseated. Suddenly he knew that his wife was starting an affair. He found out later that this sad insight was correct.

This discussion is intended to raise awareness about how deeply we affect each other in the more subtle realms. Speaking badly about others behind their backs can be almost the same as saying it in front of them when our unconscious or spiritual connections are so profound. We must be careful, then, with our words and actions to lift people's hearts to God. Right action is easy to recognize because it brings Love and connection to God. Even though it is vital to be compassionate with ourselves, and though our relationship with God is always present and available to us, relationships on the human level can be difficult to recapture if we are out of right action for too long. Once one partner reaches a certain level of detachment, regaining that love may take more patience than the couple can muster.

Usually by the time a couple breaks up or divorces, one person has known the end was approaching for so long that he or she can leave easily because his or her heart is already withdrawn from the relationship. He or she has mourned the loss of the relationship before it officially ended. Often the other person will feel as though his or her partner never loved him or her because it looks so easy to leave, and the other person appears so unwilling to work on the relationship or consider trying again. Instead this dynamic indicates that they missed the signs of their beloveds' withdrawing and detaching when the problems in the relationship went unaddressed for too long. Actually, it is easy to miss this part because it may look as though the relationship is getting better during this time. The couple is fighting less and things are more smooth between them because one person is no longer putting energy into the relationship. When one does not care about the relationship, nothing seems worth fighting about.

In fact, some marital therapists have said: "A fight a day keeps the doctor away." Though obviously too much conflict destroys many couples, if people are fighting passionately then it is likely that they still care about each other. Also, expressing one's feelings in the relationship daily decreases the build up of hurt, anger, and disappointment that leads to the kind of detachment and helplessness discussed, and prevents the resulting dissolution of the relationship. A constructive expressing of anger can "clean out the pipes" and get rid of blockages that impede the flow of intimate energies.

Game Plan

The model we are using provides other tools for handling your feelings and your beloved's besides talking about them. In healing a relationship it is important to pick your battles. If you complain about everything, your beloved will ignore you after awhile and you will not receive any of the changes you are requesting. In relationship we only have so many arrows in our pouch, so we have to use them when they count. For me, if it is possible to contain something and walk through it myself, I do. Then when something is very important for my beloved to hear, he will have all his energy available to address that concern, rather than already being overwhelmed and taxed (not to mention too frustrated with me to listen!) with ten less-important things that I have brought up in the past week.

Sometimes in the heat of the moment the emotions feel too strong to prevent yourself from acting out and hurting the relationship. Gottman, a leading researcher on relationships, watches couples fight while hooked up to all sorts of physiological monitors. He says that once people are feeling too angry or upset, they cannot think straight because they are in a state of "fight or flight." In fight or flight our blood travels away from our brains and to our large muscles so that we can attack or run from our predators. We evolved to be this way when the threats that caused this response were dangerous animals, rather than discussions with people we love! In the latter, it helps to have blood in our brain so that we can think rationally, but unfortunately we still respond with fight or flight and send our blood to our muscles.

Gottman therefore recommends taking a break from fighting when we get to this point because nothing productive will happen when we are acting from this state in which thinking clearly is physiologically improbable. Many people do not want their partners to leave during a heated argument because it makes them feel abandoned. Discussing with your beloved the adaptive nature of walking away from a fight and continuing after your heart rate returns to normal, may ease this reaction to being "left" in a heated moment.

Sometimes it helps to write yourself a letter reminding yourself what your goals are and what your game plan is for handling this situation. When you are in the issue and your mind is not working, you probably will not be able to

HEALING YOUR RELATIONSHIP

remember what you read in this book or what other techniques and resources you have for dealing with the situation. In these moments it is so soothing and re-centering to have a letter to yourself written while you were in your right mind. Give yourself plenty of time to read the letter and take it in—making yourself follow your wiser-self's advice.

I remember a letter to myself that reminded me to use my feelings for self-healing, separating them from the present situation entirely so I could explore them without blaming or thinking I had to solve the outer situation. I might have reminded myself that growing into a more loving and whole person is more important to me than anything else in this physical world, and that all these triggers are given to me to learn about where I can grow. I gave myself specific steps to follow (along the lines of the healing processes I have described) that could even be followed by someone without a lot of blood in her brain! None of my advice included stuffing my feelings, but rather feeling them fully and processing them in a way that led to my development and supported the health of the relationship. So much of healing a relationship is deep surrender, which means the self begins to die, and spiritual awakening is around the corner!

Section Three

Simple Techniques for Lasting Love

Chapter Six

Communicate Effectively

*"Excuse me if my language is poor and not enough,
But the tears of my heart,
And the crying of my soul explain more...
Your Song is sweet like honey,
No words can contain Your sweetness
Or explain the love or the real self...
I find rest in being connected,
Since love is all I aspire to...*[i]*"*

Communication, both through actions and words, bridges two hearts, creating the connection between people that gives life to the relationship. Isolation and loneliness begin where communication ceases, even if a formal bond such as marriage exists. Communication can be subtle and does not have to look like much from the outside. Perhaps both people meet on the porch at sunset and sit in silence for a while and then go back to what they were doing. As long as a mutual understanding of what that time together means, communication has occurred. The beauty in knowing and being known, and creating something larger than the self, is held here, making it the key ingredient in lasting love.

Ambiguity is the Enemy

Individuals have preferences for the types and amounts of communication they receive, so the silent sunset date could feel fulfilling for one person and leave another feeling even more lonely than when he or she is actually alone. Much of what is experienced in such a situation has to do with attributions, which we discussed earlier. If you are sitting in silence knowing that you and your beloved are sharing a moment of love and enjoying each other's presence in unspoken harmony, you can bask in the togetherness of the experience. If, on the other hand, you are imagining that your partner feels awkward and cannot think of anything to say, and that you are both aware of the painful separation in the silence, the silent sunset date has become an experience of isolation. In general, the more ambiguous the communication, the more room each person has to make attributions and create his or her own experience based on fantasy rather than reality. In other words, ambiguous communication enhances the possibility that you could be having a completely different experience of a situation than your partner.

An experience I had with one of my best friends illustrates this principle. In high school we would meet each other in the hall after our first period class. I had a serious partner at the time and felt guilty that I was not spending

COMMUNICATE EFFECTIVELY

more time with my friends. This particular friend had been writing me notes and giving them to me after class each day. One day she did not have a note for me. I wanted to make her feel valued and needed, since I had not been paying enough attention to her lately, so I said: "Where's my note? I'm going to miss it!" Her notes slowly tapered off after that and I made comments from time to time about wanting to have notes from her again. The notes did not matter to me at all, I was specifically and consciously trying to make her feel important and cared about by acting as though I liked the notes more than I did.

Perhaps a year later, when we were arguing—which was very rare—she told me that she had grown increasingly angry with me the year before when I had "expected" her to have notes for me. She felt taken for granted and used as a result of my acting as though she *should* have written me a note when I was not writing her! So, my attempt to make her feel valued was certainly not clear or direct enough, and actually made her feel less so because of the way she interpreted what I said. Decreasing the ambiguity in communication is important in making sure you and your partner are on the same page, and living in the same relationship!

If you and your beloved are indirect in your communication and often have misunderstandings, or you find yourself guessing what he or she is thinking or negatively interpreting situations or your partner's motives in doing certain things, the family motto needs to be: "Information is free!" Giving information costs you nothing, except that you may give up some of your childhood wounds that would otherwise cause you to hold back. For instance, if you are eating dinner and you think of something you need to do in the other room, announce what you are doing before you get up. Why not? Similarly, if your beloved makes a face at something you say or acts in a way that can be interpreted as hurtful, before you believe that interpretation simply ask your beloved what he or she meant by that look or that action, or what he or she was thinking or communicating.

People dislike the unknown. If you do not give the information you have, people will make up the information. For instance, if people do not know how they will do in a presentation at work, they often pretend they do, either telling themselves they are going to do poorly, or telling themselves they will do great. People often make negative future predictions, so rather than feeling anxious about the unknown, they end up feeling even more anxious about something negative they have decided will happen. Similarly, we act as though we can read each other's minds by seeing one little facial expression on our beloved and thinking things like: "She's angry with me," or "He does not like the way I am dressed." Many times mind-reading causes a problem that did not exist—we are having our feelings in relation to unreality[xv].

I remember when my college partner and I would spend our summers away from each other geographically. We wrote and called regularly. One time he had not contacted me or returned my calls for much longer than usual. I

COMMUNICATE EFFECTIVELY

thought he had probably met someone else at the summer camp at which he was working. I wrote him an angry letter telling him how hurt I was and that he needed to communicate with me. I asked my mother to read the letter before I sent it (she happens to be a psychologist). She asked me why I was so upset that we had not had contact if the last contact we had had was positive; so as far as I knew things were great between us. I told her he did not care enough to call and was probably seeing someone else. When she asked what evidence I had for this belief, I could not come up with any besides not having heard from him. She advised me to brainstorm other possible scenarios and not to send the letter yet. Though I had not come up with this possibility in my brainstorming, when my partner called to tell me he had been very sick and in the hospital (and missed me so much of course!), I was very glad that I had not sent my letter.

So, when we are on the receiving end of ambiguous communication we must ask questions to gather more information, rather than make assumptions. If we are on the offering side, give as much clear information as possible so that your beloved will not misinterpret what you say or do. As a rule with the "information is free!" motto, never give one-word answers. Always offer extra information and build on a question to further the conversation and share yourself. It is our human tendency to want people to read our minds, but in truth the way to be known is to tell people who you are and what you need. So many couples do not ask each other for what they want and become upset when their partners do not give it. As infants we could not communicate our needs verbally and had to rely on our caregivers to read our minds. This dynamic leaves such a deep mark, especially if your caregivers did not understand your cries. Even a 2-4 year old often believes that if mother loved him, she would read his mind. Many people feel that love is not proven until their partners know their unspoken desires and thoughts. Making this process conscious may help you care for the infant inside that wants to be known without saying a word, while in the adult world you are able to give the necessary information to have your desires met and have a fulfilling relationship.

Verbal & Nonverbal Communication

Let's examine how verbal and nonverbal communication can be used in ways that serve the relationship. If the saying "actions speak louder than words" is true, we especially want to use actions when our feelings or intentions are positive. When you feel loving toward your partner or have the intention to change a behavior that hurts him or her, you want to communicate this respect and caring in the most potent way—through action. Give your beloved the experience of being loved, rather than only telling him or her this fact. Many couples complain that their partners are always saying "I love you," or "I'm sorry," but not acting as though these are true. Those kind words help the relationship if the words are sincere, but loving actions build your partner's trust in your words and make them more effective in opening your beloved's heart.

COMMUNICATE EFFECTIVELY

Verbal and nonverbal relating go hand in hand in effective communication. So, though actions build trust in words and illustrate feelings potently, actions without words are similar to writing papers and not signing your name to them. You have accomplished the most difficult part (changing behaviors or doing acts of kindness usually requires more effort than saying a few sentences) so why not highlight it and drive your point home? A friend's husband works very hard and contributes a lot to the family, but he does not tell her that he is doing it *for her* because he loves her. That last piece is effortless, yet makes the behavior vastly more meaningful and fulfilling for the recipient. Similarly, if you are working on changing something that hurts your partner, you might say: "I have been working hard not to _____, because I know it bothers you. I care so much about you and your feelings about the relationship. I think I am doing it a lot less now."

The statement "actions speak louder than words" is even truer when applied to expressing negative feelings. When what you want to express is possibly hurtful to the relationship, it is better to use words than to act out your feelings. Acting out communicates so potently, and often ambiguously, that it can severely undermine relationships and not even get across the point. If you give your beloved the silent treatment when you are angry, for instance, you make a strong negative emotional impact on your beloved without helping him or her understand what went awry. Gottman calls ignoring your partner "stonewalling" and his research shows it is one of the most destructive behaviors in a relationship. Other examples of acting out feelings include slamming doors, physical or emotional abuse, stomping away or pushing your partner away, mean or exasperated facial expressions, etc. It is doing whatever your feelings tell you to do--following your emotional impulses to action.

Talking about feelings, in contrast, allows people to remain on the same team as they work to understand each other and solve the problem together. It is so important to realize that feelings do not mean action. You can be violently angry or deeply hurt and have a calm, constructive conversation about it. When you are not suppressing feelings or acting them out, you can explore them and learn from them. Many people are scared of their emotions or their partner's emotions because they do not realize that feeling something does not mean you have to act upon it. You merely learn to relate to your feelings as a loving adult, rather than allow the tantruming child inside to take over. Talk about the child rather than acting like him or her!

A difference exists between observing feelings and being IN them. When you are inside the feeling you see the world through the feeling only and lose the rational part of yourself because you have entirely believed what the feeling is telling you. Observing the feeling allows you to have the feeling without squelching it, but you can explore it as a part of you and stay in your rational self looking at the emotion from there. Naming your impulses ("I feel like throwing something!") and describing your physical sensations ("My stomach is in knots and my heart is racing") can help you develop this observing self and talk about your feelings rather than live in or from them.

Exploring vs. Explaining

A further distinction to make, once you are talking about your feelings rather than acting them out, is whether you are exploring or explaining. Exploring may look like what was just described—noticing sensations, impulses, thoughts, and all different aspects of what is going on inside you with curiosity about it. Explaining, in contrast, is telling a story about what you are experiencing. It might be a re-telling of who said what or an explanation of why you think you are upset. Explaining is stating what you already know, while exploring is a process of self-discovery and naturally develops the observing self and decreases acting out. It is also much easier to join someone who is exploring than it is to join someone who is explaining. Has your beloved ever said: "Yes, your telling of the story is completely correct and I learned something from having you tell your side of what happened?" Mine hasn't! Instead, he or she probably argues with your perspective if you are emotionally aroused and explaining. Exploring, however, is an open door for your partner to empathize or at least be involved in the process of learning about you and supporting you without feeling attacked[xvi].

In fact, if you explore, very often you will find that you and your partner are experiencing the same thing, giving you something to come together around. For instance, you might say: "I feel hurt and my stomach feels tight." Your beloved may be feeling exactly the same way. Already, then, you and your beloved are in the same boat and perhaps will be wise enough to care for each other and have true empathy and connection around the pain. If each of you relay your story (explaining), however, disagreement is stimulated. If the two of you saw the situation the same way, the conflict most likely would not have occurred in the first place.

Navigating Similarity & Difference

If you want your beloved to understand something new, why not go straight to the differences and argue them out? Little productive communication is likely to occur this way. People seem to despise difference and when faced with it will close up to protect themselves from change. This defense allows a person to preserve the way one is. The process happens naturally, even if the person does not like himself or herself and would rather change. Our drive to preserve things familiar and stable is so strong that closing (or using whatever defenses we have, such as arguing) is almost automatic when faced with too much difference.

The process of human development involves accepting and integrating differences so that we can all become more complex, and therefore evolved and mature[xvii]. The optimal amount of new information leads to growth without destabilizing the system in an overwhelming way. The way to facilitate working productively with differences is to join around similarity first. People are most likely to loosen their boundaries and not have the instinctual defenses to difference if they feel connected to someone and similar to him or her before being exposed to the differences.

COMMUNICATE EFFECTIVELY

Rather than saying: "I thought we decided not to wear shoes in the house and you always do it anyway and make such a mess! Stop doing that," you might say: "Hmmm...It sure is convenient to be able to wear shoes in the house, especially when you are in and out so often while doing projects outside. I do it sometimes too. I'm still aware of the benefits of taking them off before coming in, though, so maybe we should discuss it again and weigh the pros and cons." The saying: "Step on one side of ambivalence and the other side flares up" seems to capture how unproductive it is to argue one side strongly if you are trying to reach agreement or understanding with someone.

So, introducing difference slowly can prevent the strong defenses against it that block communication. Many people define themselves largely by how they are different from others, even though similarities give as much useful information about oneself. When we emphasize difference in relationships we risk becoming increasingly polarized around those differences. For example, one person might start out somewhat more responsible than the other. If the person complains a lot about being the responsible one and the other person being irresponsible, both people begin embracing these roles more and more. The less responsible one may have trouble trying to be more responsible when his or her responsible actions are going to go unnoticed by his or her partner, and the responsible partner is handling everything that needs to be taken care of anyway! So, the complexity that belongs in each person (a responsible part and a lax part) is instead held in the relationship, each person taking one part or the other. Recognizing similarities helps prevent this painful dynamic. If this sort of polarization already exists, noticing exceptions to the rule (when is the irresponsible person acting responsibly and vice versa?) can slowly undo these roles.

Unfortunately, in arguments couples tend to exaggerate their feelings and present their perspectives dramatically, heightening the perceived difference. It is a good idea to take this into account and learn to automatically translate "always" or "never" in a fight to mean "often" and "rarely" rather than try to prove to your beloved that you do not *always* do that, etc. Couples may allow themselves to become distracted by these particulars so that they can argue about an outer detail rather than the deeper issues that need addressing. For instance, perhaps you were originally communicating your desire for attention or affection, but you used the example that he or she "never" asks you about your day. Then your partner will of course give counter examples and now you are arguing about whether or not he or she ever asks you about your day, rather than exploring your important feeling of wanting to be shown more love.

==Remember to stop frequently in arguments and ask if what you are fighting about at that moment is significant to you—is it worth it to win? If you prove he or she *never* asks you how your day is, versus that he or she rarely asks, does that gain you anything?== These hang-ups are the reason why exploring instead of explaining is so vital in healthy communication. First connecting around the experience before gently introducing the outer reasons for the pain or

COMMUNICATE EFFECTIVELY

anger increases the likelihood that the different perspectives on the situation will actually be heard and processed so that appropriate adjustments can be made. Many couples become trapped in cycles of the same conflict indefinitely because neither one is willing to truly hear the other person's perspective and understand something new.

Perhaps awareness of the human fear of change and resistance to taking in a different view will help you battle this tendency and really listen to your partner. It will feel counter-intuitive because the exact moment to focus on understanding the different perspective is the moment in which you most want to fight back and defend your own. The stakes are high, however, because much pain is caused by repeatedly reliving these patterns. In addition, our spiritual development prospers as we grow more complex by accepting and integrating differences. We become less attached to a limited (though comfortable to our egos) view of reality and contain more potential for peace inside and out.

When you want to really join your beloved and open his or her heart, you can begin with simple reflective statements to show you heard and understood. As infants we began to know ourselves through what was reflected back to us by others. We would say: "Goo Goo!" and hopefully some adult would mimic our expression and tone and say back lovingly: "Goo Goo!" Through this mirroring over time we learn who we are and slowly internalize that sense of self to form our identity as a separate being. If this process is thwarted, many issues with boundaries, confusion about who one is, and conflict in relationships can result. Lack of early mirroring can cause such a need to be validated from the outside world that without it a person falls apart. Even when we have good caregivers, we are all still hard-wired at some level to long to be known, making it so fulfilling when those we care about really "get" us and can demonstrate it.

Early on in graduate school to become a psychologist I was learning basic therapy skills. I paired up to practice reflecting back to a partner what he or she shared with me. Though the research shows how deeply healing this aspect of therapy is, I wanted to skip ahead to more advanced techniques. I was shocked, however, at how comforting and relieving it felt when I shared some minor struggle with my classmate and she stated back to me exactly what I had said. She was not trying to be or sound particularly empathic, make an interpretation of what I was saying, or offer an insight. She literally repeated back to me, with clear attention to me and to my concern, exactly what I had said. I never again minimized the power of true listening and of showing someone that you heard and understood. It is an enormous gift to give to your beloved, especially when you give it in a heated moment when you are tempted to fight instead.

Slowing It Down

One way to slow down to help yourself act with more thoughtfulness, is to have the discussion through writing. One person writes what he or she wants to say to the other and then the other person writes his or her response back. On important or difficult topics, you may agree ahead of time to use this method. You will also have time while your partner is writing to do remembrance and stay focused on Love, perhaps praying for real communication and healing to occur and then opening to receive the help and guidance that comes. Recall that when you receive guidance from God you are listening as deeply in your heart as possible to see what your heart moves you to do and how. If the place in your heart has God's qualities, such as peace, compassion, or a sense of lightness, then you can trust and follow.

When you are in remembrance you can also test things before saying them to see how your beloved will respond. Energetically hold the statement you want to make and then gently place it in your beloved's heart. Watch from your level of deep knowing to see how the heart responds. When you are in remembrance and alignment with God—feeling that connection deep inside—you will perceive things in your own way. Some people see visually. For instance, you may see an image that closes or rejects, or an image showing opening and receptivity. Or, you may hear or feel physical sensations, or simply know. If you want to know God, you must discover how He communicates with you and feel how and when He moves your heart. In terms of choosing what to say in important conversations with your beloved, if you get the sense that what you would like to say will not be received, simply change some words to find wording his or her heart can accept. When the right words come or your heart is in the right place with what you are trying to communicate, you will feel an opening.

Couples can practice a structured back and forth communication in their daily lives to increase intimacy and prevent future conflicts[xviii]. The structure is similar to that described in the previous chapter when discussing how to take turns listening or playing the healer role in fights to facilitate communication and healing. Using this process in an argument is actually the test, and you can prepare for the test by practicing regularly in minor conflicts or simply while sharing yourselves with each other. One person's job is to speak and the other person's job is to listen. Allow plenty of time for the speaker to communicate whatever he or she wants to have heard and the listener to hear it and accurately reflect what he or she heard. The process of the listener understanding what was communicated may take 10 minutes or longer.

Do not switch roles right after the first session, but instead come back at a later time to allow the other person be the speaker. This break protects the listener from the tendency to think about what he or she would like to say back. When listening, you try to hear what your beloved says completely in the context of him or her, with no reference back to self. The listener does not defend himself or herself and never argues with the other's perception. In fact, the goal is to listen until you prove the other person *right!* Since we cannot change another person's perception, the way to move forward in a relationship is to truly understand that perception. When we take responsibility for

COMMUNICATE EFFECTIVELY

another person's feelings we can quickly feel inadequate because we cannot fix them or because we blame ourselves. This process usually leads to defensiveness to protect ourselves from this experience. So, it is best to focus on being responsive to, but not responsible for, our beloveds' feelings. Be especially careful with questions. They are good to help you clarify and guide the speaker deeper, but do not use them as indirect criticism or to highlight inaccuracies in what your beloved is saying.

The speaker's goal is to share his or her feelings only for the purpose of being understood, not to change the other person or hurt him or her. First the speaker can describe the emotion and attach it to a person or experience. The speaker can include how this issue makes him or her feel about him or herself. Then the speaker can link his or her present feelings to the past outside of the present relationship or trigger, discovering and exploring the deeper roots of why something was so upsetting and detaching it from the current situation. At the end, the speaker can ask the listener what he or she heard, if it has not been reflected back already.

It can be an effective tool to audiotape or videotape these interactions. This way you can go back and watch how you did and identify from the outside your strengths and weaknesses in effective communication. Also, being taped encourages both parties to try harder to maintain the structure and to communicate with love. Ultimately, the reason to give up defenses, criticism, and uncontained anger is that they just do not work. The only thing that works is to become interested in truly understanding your partner.

People love those who care about them. Plus, in understanding your partner you understand yourself as well, as we choose partners who unconsciously complement us in profound ways.

It is important to keep what your beloved shares with you close to your heart and be careful about sharing it with others or bringing it up later in contexts that could make him or her uncomfortable. The intimacy you are building is based on trust. Using the information exchanged to later hurt the person or prove a point against him or her is a betrayal that would tremendously undermine the relationship. You want to behave in ways that encourage each other to share and trust more. The kind of personal communication that builds intimacy should happen regularly to keep your love forever growing and deepening. You and your beloved may set aside time weekly to share your dreams and what has been on your mind, including things that are bothering you in the relationship. My parents, who have been married for thirty-five years, fondly recall the scheduled weekly meetings they would have early on in their marriage where they would bring their "best selves" to discuss how the relationship was going and say things that were difficult to say. Remember that information is free and you can't have a relationship without allowing yourself to be known, and putting effort into knowing your beloved as well.

Chapter Seven

Water Your Tree

"The life of beloveds is for each to be holy, and to care about one another. This relationship is like a holy tree whose roots grow deep into the earth, and the earth is the heart of God. How do you nourish this tree? By giving it love and clean water; water that has been cleansed of all the troubles of this world. It is necessary for the tree to grow strong in order to give shade to all the lovers of God who are beneath it. When nourished, her roots will grow deep into the earth, becoming all the qualities of God, covering the universe with His essence. This is the Tree of Life and it is necessary for it to be nourished with the love of God. Then it will give the holiest of fruits with His permission and have the sweetest flowers, because it comes from one source.[vii]"

Being Known

Practicing the healing and communication techniques described are the central tools in maintaining lasting love. Let's explore a mix of other concepts and tips, however, which will further support you in nourishing your relationship. To begin, remember that one of the most basic human desires is to be cared about and known. Couples should always have their eyes on this fact and try to give each other this deeply-sought experience. Being known is not a one-time occurrence where you can prove you really know the person and then the other person's desire is satisfied. We long to be known moment to moment—which means people must be aware of us and understand and accept that person of whom they are aware.

First, therefore, it is vital to show you are thinking of your partner, whether or not he or she is present. If your beloved mentioned needing something at the grocery store that morning and you pick it up on the way home, for instance, you have not only demonstrated caring about meeting his or her needs, but (perhaps even more importantly!) you have shown you remembered that all day and were therefore thinking about him or her. The same concept would be true if you call after work to ask if he or she needs you to pick up anything on the way home. This act shows a consciousness that your beloved is in your life, important to you, and on your mind.

Second, you can demonstrate that not only is your partner in your mind and heart, but you deeply know him or her. So, continuing with our grocery store example, if you think that your beloved usually takes about a week to run out of apples, and it has been about that long since either of you shopped, and you know he or she really loves apples and would be sad not to have them for breakfast the next morning, then you may stop and pick up apples without having to call. Or, if you know your beloved has a stressful

WATER YOUR TREE

day at work and is relaxed by a clean house, candle light, or a call from you during the day, then you try to create that relaxing experience for your partner that day in particular. This process shows you were thinking of the fact that today was especially stressful for him or her, you knew what would be supportive for your beloved because you know him or her so well, and you cared enough to do something about it. It is thoughtful to give your partner flowers, but it will be experienced as much more meaningful and fulfilling if you have also chosen your beloved's favorite kind of flowers and given them in a moment when you know your beloved would most appreciate it. All of these details give your partner the important experience not only of being cherished, but of being *known*.

Several of my clients who tend to be disorganized lament how their partners gave them planners for their birthdays. The gift is more of a hint of what is lacking than a present that shows the partner knows and loves the person as he or she is. In this case, the present demonstrates knowing the person, but does not communicate acceptance and celebration of that. Similarly, for Christmas some parents I know gave their artistic, dyslexic daughter an investment account to manage stocks. It led to her crying and feeling overwhelmed. It could be argued that parents have the right to be as much in touch with what the child needs to learn as they are in touch with who the child actually is because of the parents' responsibility to prepare the child for the world. As a partner, however, if you are always trying to lead your beloved in a particular direction, it will cause resentment, a sense of lack of freedom and respect, and possibly rebellion.

Acceptance

You knew who your partner was when you decided to be with him or her. Many people marry people they see as "fixer-uppers" partly because of our tendency to recreate the dynamics of our families of origin, even if they were unhealthy and hurt us. As discussed, we often unconsciously choose someone similar to our parents who never gave us some aspect of the relationship we wanted, so that we can solve the problem and prove we are worthy of love or capable of overcoming the original issue. Of course, if we have chosen well then our partners are equally resistant to development in that area as was the parent with whom we struggled, because we are actually scared to have things any other way, as that is all we have ever known.

In these complex patterns, we simultaneously need that dynamic and unconsciously like it because of the familiarity, but also suffer the pain from it and think we are trying to resolve it. For instance, a woman whose father was emotionally unavailable may choose relationships with men who are also unavailable so that she assures that the dynamic she knows will continue. At the same time she is tormented by their inconsistency and is driven to reach them emotionally so she can conquer and solve the childhood problem and prove she was enough to merit her father's attention. She has chosen, of course, men with whom she will never succeed in accomplishing this goal, assuring the continued comfort of the dynamic she knows. This portrayal may seem hopeless, but psychotherapy effectively addresses and changes these dynamics regularly, and so can you. People are very resilient once they understand what is happening and feel supported in developing beyond it. The unconscious childhood dynamics that are stimulated by our partners are a large reason why the most painful parts of our relationships can teach us the most about ourselves and point us toward the places where we need healing.

In terms of our beloved's upsetting behavior, we have heard the words "no one is perfect" so many times for a reason. Where you can possibly be accepting, do. Many partners do not consider change until the other person ends the relationship and says it is because of that behavior. Once that point is reached, however, the relationship usually cannot be recovered because the person who leaves has already closed the door emotionally. If they do come back together, damage to the feeling of safety and commitment has occurred. You can, however, still support the growth that your beloved desires without making it your project, or a necessity for you that he or she changes. The most effective way to change people is to lose interest in changing them and focus on understanding them and them understanding you[vi]. Of course, we are speaking about the day-to-day relationship here. From time to time something important will emerge where you will be asking for a change from your beloved for your sake, but this scenario should be far from the norm. People need space to be free to be anyone they want and to discover from their own hearts into whom they want to develop.

A spiritual perspective on relationships includes being a clean tablet on which God can write, whether about how your beloved should be, or about how your life should go in general. If you have already decided what a moment should bring or hold, you have not only set yourself up for an emotional reaction if it does not happen that way, but also possibly closed yourself off from some better scenario that would have occurred if you had been more open. When you are in relationship with the Divine, be expectant of a plan or experience more perfect than the one you can create. This plan may take you through some territory you would have rather avoided, but it leads somewhere finer than where you would have taken yourself. Not attaching to ideas you create, but instead staying open to a greater inspiration or direction, is integral in allowing your spirit to blossom and run your life. If you can see the Divine in whatever happens, and stay in a place of receptivity, you can view your relationship through your heart rather than your mind and begin to actualize a spiritual perspective on relationships.

Acknowledging and accepting each other's preferences in connection style also helps the relationship fulfill both people. Robert Steinburg, an influential social scientist, proposes three central desires for different kinds of people: passion, intimacy, and commitment. Passion can be the sexual/sensual, or the fun, enlivening, exciting, or dramatic aspects of relating. Some people crave this kind of passion and seek it as a primary facet of their relationships. Intimacy

WATER YOUR TREE

is deeply knowing your partner as we have been discussing, and sharing emotional closeness and engagement with each other. Different people are comfortable with different levels of intimacy, which we will discuss more later. Commitment is a construct describing the kind of people who stand by each other, and do not mind if they live parallel lives as long as they have the other person there. In other words, a couple strongly valuing this construct might be able to eat a meal together in silence and find that fulfilling.

People can desire any combination of passion, intimacy, and commitment from a relationship, and sometimes they are all equally important to a person. Many times, however, a person views a relationship as primarily consisting of one or two of these constructs and does not greatly value the other(s). Relationships that work easily often consist of a match between people in terms of which of these aspects of a relationship are important to each person. People are often, however, mismatched in this way. One person is looking for passion, for instance, while the other seeks intimacy. These situations make it especially important to accept your partner and be able to provide what he or she values in a relationship in addition to seeking what you value.

In some ways, maintaining a healthy, deeply loving relationship, comes down to both partners asking themselves: "What makes the *other* person happy and fulfilled, and are they receiving it?" Then really explore how you could provide what lightens and supports the other person's spirit. You can take some time to sit in your heart and ask to understand what is needed and how to give it, just as you do in healing. A simple hint, however, is to watch how your beloved gives to you (which may or may not be the way you most prefer, but is probably how he or she would most like to receive) and give to your partner in that way.

One caveat to this process is that sometimes partners seek something unhealthy because of past pain. A man who grew up with a mother who was always disappearing, for instance, may feel that love is a relationship in which he seeks a woman and can't find her consistently. If you play this role you will provide that for which the person's mind is unconsciously looking (and trying to elicit from you), but will never teach him what true Love is. As you know, we unconsciously prefer that with which we are familiar (it is comfortable and we know how to do it) and those childhood states to which we bonded, so it will take valiant work to overcome these preferences. If you feel your partner wanting something to recreate an unhealthy pattern from the past, go beyond that, into who your beloved is underneath, so that you find his or her true need.

Sometimes you have to go deep into your beloved's heart to find out what he or she really seeks because the actions on the outside show something else. Or, maybe your beloved can articulate what is desired, but actively repels it when you give it, or elicits something else from you energetically or through actions. You can cut through all of this confusing outer level by aligning yourself with Truth and keeping your eyes on that. Make plenty of space for yourself to feel your own heart and from there ask to be shown what is really right to give and how to give it in a way that can be received. When you feel true guidance you can ignore the dynamics that would otherwise pull you into a dysfunctional cycle, and simply continue to reach your beloved's real heart. You should also contemplate your own dynamics in terms of what you seek on an outer and an inner level from your beloved and how you might thwart the process of receiving it for whatever reason.

A level exists at which we all need different things to heal based on our own unique childhood pain. Beneath that layer, however, is a level at which we all seek the same things, which is where this discussion began. Therefore, if you ever feel lost as to how to be with your partner in the right way, you can always return to your own deepest heart and feel what partner you would like to have. Then, be that partner for your beloved.

Discernment

As you can see, feeding your relationship can be extremely complex in the fine-tuning, but it can also be very simple when you feel you cannot contain the complexity. To paraphrase an ancient Sufi saying: "Leave that which makes you doubt for that which does not." In any interaction with your beloved, feel your options and choose the one with which your heart feels the most okay. This process can take place from moment to moment, as in a waltz where your heart is your dance partner. You feel your heart's leaning and then immediately follow, from a sway in one direction to a twirling step in another, seamlessly finding the most right or beautiful path for each breath.

If you have more time or an important decision to make, you can go through this process in slow motion. Find a comfortable place to sit, perhaps placing your hand over the center of your chest and slightly bowing your head so that you remember the heart is taking the lead. Then spend as long as you need to feel from your heart each of your options, one at a time. Notice the world that opens when you think of going in a particular direction. Is it light or dark? Does it bring up a subtle feeling of some kind—pleasant or not? Do you feel anxious or clear when you sit with this option? Once you have felt how your heart relates to each alternative, you can do remembrance, calling upon God to show you His perspective on it. Simply feel your being relaxing into the ocean of Love and look out from the purest place of holiness, peace, freedom, or caring you find inside.

From that place notice how each of your options looks and feels. Pay attention to what images, colors, sounds, words, or feelings come to you with each. From all of this data you can feel from your heart which of your options feels right. If you are still confused, you can stay in your remembrance and imagine each of your options lined up in front of your body. As you say the name of God, see and feel light coming through the name, through your heart, and flowing toward one of your options. See where the light goes! When you have chosen right, you feel almost a sigh of relief in your being—as though something relaxes. If you do not receive an answer right away, continue sincerely asking your questions and be patient, trusting your direction will become more clear over time. Sometimes we are not conscious of the understanding we are given when we ask, but it will still affect us without our knowing it.

Having a process to receive Divine guidance, whether it is this process or some other you know, seems so critical in weaving your spirituality into your relationship. A book cannot answer every question about your personal situation, but the Real Knower and Lover can. Do you confront your beloved about this or that? Do you confront him or her now or later? What do you say when you do so? How do you ignite your beloved's passion for you? Why are you scared of intimacy? Is it time to have children? What should you do when your beloved pushes your patience beyond its capacity? Your heart has all the answers through the generous spring God has put deep inside. You just have to remember to go to the watering hole and drink!

Neediness

Why must we go to the Source to quench our thirst? We are innately needy. Though this thought causes many people to cringe, I think upon reflection most would realize it is true. Every moment we depend on the earth for our very next breath, without which we could not live. Humans spend so much time trying to be self-sufficient that we ignore the spiritual banquet available in our hearts and search for food everywhere else! I think one reason we are repelled by neediness is because we have searched for fulfillment where it can't be found, and come to believe it does not exist. It is certainly not a good thing to be needy when what you need is not available, so most choose to pretend they are not needy to protect themselves from the pain of not receiving. When we search outside our connection with God to try to fulfill the desires of our heart, we fail.

This search for fulfillment where it cannot be found may be the reason why people perceived as "needy" are often turned away or rejected by lovers or potential lovers. People innately know that they will never be able to satiate the source of another person's neediness, because the true neediness is for God. We want to avoid the inevitable experience of inadequacy that would result if we undertook the impossible task of meeting a person's needs when he or she thinks we are their source of nourishment, and so we are naturally repelled. The answer is not to avoid or deny our own neediness! Instead, look to the One who can actually satiate the place inside that is crying for something more. We must accept our neediness, know that it is not neediness for what the world has to offer, and go to God over and over for real sustenance.

This understanding may help in addressing both your own needs and your beloved's. For yourself you may hold in mind that it is not your beloved's job to suffice you. If your beloved is repelled by you when you are in a needy state, spend time in remembrance and find the place of Sustenance inside before you approach your beloved. You will ironically then be much more likely to also receive what you want from your beloved and the outside world. Your beloved may hide all of his or her needs, or may bring them all to you. Either way, knowing you are merely a conduit to provide to your beloved whatever moves through your heart from the Divine frees you from the burden of his or her need and makes giving an experience in which you are receiving as well as giving.

When the outside world is not providing what we need, we are simply being pointed inward to the Source. God also gives to us so richly through the outer, however, and must want us to be able to receive from the world as well. In doing so, be sure to practice diffused dependency. In other words, we all have dependency needs and these needs only become unhealthy when we place them all on one person or on a few people. Spread out your needs over a large group so that you all support each other a little and no person holds too much of the responsibility for giving to you. Of course the true dependency is on the Divine, but if you are someone who feels the Divine most easily through being with other people, simply cast your net widely so that many people can share in holding your heart, not just your beloved.

The Dance of Closeness & Separation

Related to neediness versus independence, individuals enjoy different levels of closeness based on their past experiences in relationships. Everyone has some familiarity with losing oneself in someone else and then becoming separate, at a minimum from when we were babies. We began without perception of other, and lived in a world of unity with our surroundings as infants. We slowly grew to see that we are separate, eventually differentiating ourselves to various extents from our mothers and/or fathers. We can see a baby developing separation very clearly as it reaches the toddler stage (the "terrible two's").

We all have different experiences, however, of how the closeness and separation felt, and what was comfortable or modeled for us in our families of origin. Two people can cope very differently with the same situation growing up and those survival strategies will greatly influence their preferences in future relationships. With mothers who are overbearing and suffocating, for instance, some children strongly withdraw or rebel to keep from losing themselves, thereby becoming difficult to reach and suspicious of allowing anyone close, while others attain love by being what the mother desires, thereby developing a lasting need for that kind of dependency. Most relationships have a dance of closeness and separateness that moves in and out as the ocean tides. Without conscious internal work on it, however, an individual's preferred location along this continuum seems consistent over time, or consistently shifts between two strategies (wanting a high level of closeness but then shutting down and becoming unreachable if he or she does not get the closeness, for instance).

To summarize the closeness-separateness dance, some people maintain a lot of distance with their lovers and feel they will be consumed and destroyed if they become too close—they will lose themselves or get hurt. They become claustrophobic with too much intimacy. I've heard people

WATER YOUR TREE

joke that the best sex is after a fight. Why? The distance created by the fight allows some people to feel safer merging with another person during lovemaking. Others feel the most safe with a high level of closeness, almost moving as one person with their beloveds. Distance may feel as though the relationship is falling apart and is unfulfilling—like trying to warm oneself with fire by standing across the room from it. Relationships can be easier when both members of a couple have similar preferences for their levels of closeness and separateness. Most of us, however, have some issues around abandonment, envelopment, or both.

Often one person will take one role—really needing the other person and fearing abandonment—while the other person will take the other role—scared of the neediness of the other and trying to gain distance to avoid being consumed. Sometimes these roles switch back and forth between the partners because one elicits the other. Society seems to encourage men to fear envelopment and women to fear abandonment, potentially influencing how this dance often happens in a gender-stereotyped way. Men are generally seen as less comfortable with feelings than women, which could also be tied to this dynamic of managing closeness. To the extent men fear envelopment they would want to hide feelings because that sharing would increase intimacy. Women, in contrast, would particularly want their partners to share their feelings because it gives them more information about what is going on inside the other person, soothing their fear of being abandoned.

When your and your beloved's desires along this continuum conflict, whether or not it happens in a gender-stereotyped way, perhaps you can see it as a door to important spiritual development. This conflict points to deep fundamental issues such as trust and the ability to receive, stemming back to very early childhood and our basic needs as humans. You can use the spiritual healing techniques we have explored to turn to God in the place that fears annihilation or being left, so that you can feel the steadfast nature of Spirit and become more reliant on that. ==Learning to be comfortable at both ends of the closeness-separateness continuum and able to move between the two without too much emotional turbulence will free you to engage in life more fully and playfully, with less fear.== It feels okay to be very intimate, yet okay to be distant. Either way you have a felt sense of the solidity of the relationship and the solidity of your own independence.

Cognitions & Context

Being able to navigate this dance, and the other day-to-day challenges of your relationship, rests partly in how you think about what is happening. If your beloved seems distant, for instance, you could think: "He's angry at me," or "She does not care about how I am doing." Or, you might think: "She has had a long day at work and needs time to rest before connecting with me," or "He's loving me from afar—this is how they did it in his family." You can see how different these statements to yourself would make you feel.

So, yes, you have a relationship with your beloved that may need attention, but you also have a relationship with yourself that is active at every moment. How you talk to yourself reflects the health of this relationship—do you relate to yourself as a good mom or a bad mom, for instance? When you make a mistake do you encourage yourself or reprimand yourself? If your relationship with yourself is not loving, it is difficult to experience the world, or even God, as loving either.

It would be interesting to read this book again with your relationship with yourself as the focus, so YOU are your beloved. You would probably find that putting energy into that relationship would make the largest difference in your experience of life, and would greatly affect your romantic relationship as well. Part of having a healthy relationship with yourself is understanding that you exist within a set of contexts, so you do not need to take things just personally[xix]. All of us are faced with hundreds of opportunities to take things just personally every day, and can instead choose to recognize the many contexts in which we are operating moment to moment.

For instance, I was in a study group recently in which we spent a long time laughing. Afterward someone said that they felt the laughing had prevented us from being as productive as we could have. Another group member's feelings were very hurt by this comment. She thought it meant that people in the group did not like her because she had started the laughing. That perspective is taking things just personally. The context, on the other hand, was that the person who said laughing was not our most productive time was trying to make our future groups more beneficial, not making a commentary on the character or worthiness of anyone in the group. Also, almost everyone in the group had been laughing, so laughing was not about this one person, but about everyone.

If you have a friendly relationship with yourself, you would tend to remember the context and understand the comment was not about you. If you are waiting to find fault with yourself, however, blinders seem to prevent context from neutralizing the experience so that instead you see it as completely about you. With a beloved it is so critical to hold context constantly in mind. If your beloved is being impatient with you, is he hungry? Is she tired? Did something stressful happen at work? Now, yes, maybe you are involved in some way. Perhaps you forgot to call and say what time you were going to be home. But, even then, consider context. It is not just that you forgot to call, it is that her mother never remembered her at all growing up, making your not calling particularly painful. You are never operating outside the bounds of context.

Key Moments

Awareness of context also helps you recognize important moments in your relationship where trying extra hard will reward you tenfold. For instance, if your beloved loses a parent and is in a period of suffering, your patience will make a deep, lasting, emotional impression on your beloved. When push comes to shove, are you there? For instance, my parents tell a story about hiking in Colorado early on in their marriage. As they were breaking camp my mother brushed her teeth by a stream and left her retainer (for maintaining straight teeth) on the stream bank. After hiking the rest of the day up hill they were exhausted as they neared a place to set up camp. A storm was rolling in and it had started to rain.

My mother was horrified when she realized she had left her retainer behind. At the time they did not have the money to just leave it and get a new one later. She was so nervous to tell my father. When she finally did, he paused, internally processed that he was the logical one to retrieve it, and then said: "Okay! I'll run down and get it." He could have complained or made her feel guilty for leaving it, but he probably would have ended up going back to get it anyway. The outer outcome for him, then, would have been the same either way. His preventing himself from saying a single negative thing about it in a moment that was vulnerable for my mother, however, had a profound positive effect on their relationship. My mother said it solidified something inside her about her deep love for him and trust in him as a partner, and the appreciation she felt lasted for a long time—maybe a lifetime, as the story is still with her and was told to me. He returned to camp at bedtime, soaking wet, but what he gained in his relationship was priceless.

Similarly, the week of my wedding I was extremely busy handling what seemed like hundreds of details. From the stress of all that I had to do, I felt more emotionally taxed than usual. My fiancé loved the car he had at the time, and had performed all sorts of cleaning and detailing on it to have it perfect for all the guests who were coming. Two days before the wedding, on my way rushing out to do something or other, I backed into his car and smashed the front end. I gasped when I heard the crushing car sound. I knew he would be crushed too. I held my breath as I ran back inside to tell him what happened. He did not blink an eye or make any expression, but just nodded and said with an accepting tone: "Okay." In his calm, loving, we'll-take-care-of-it response, I felt exactly what it was that I loved about him, and still love about him. Those moments make a lasting impression. ==Consider the larger picture when you respond to your beloved, especially when he or she is in a vulnerable spot and your reaction has power to make an impact.== It might feel like a good moment to make a point about being more careful or not being absent-minded, but it could be a much more powerful opportunity to build love and trust. Why waste it?

Responsiveness

Let's broaden this discussion to the more everyday interaction and how we impact the climate of our relationship by the subtleties of how we relate. How you engage with people enormously affects what you get back from them. This statement is true not only in a tit for tat kind of way—you have to give to receive—but also in terms of whether or not you naturally bring out your beloved's best self. As a teacher I have been amazed at how much the quality of my lectures are affected by how students are responding to me. At one community college, I was floored by how difficult it was to teach because my students looked disinterested and annoyed before I even started (of course this perception of them is a mind-read, as discussed earlier, based on the ambiguous stimuli of blank faces—I do not know what they were actually thinking or feeling). At the University of Iowa, however, the students appeared to adore my class and greeted me with eagerness and questions. I, in turn, was my best self and earned further excitement from them, continuing a positive cycle.

In teaching to a blank-faced audience, it was a huge victory if I succeeded in enlivening the group because they had preemptively created a teacher who felt a subtle sense of hopelessness and dismay underneath what she was saying. I noticed my mind did not work as well, which is a response to negative or no feedback that has been demonstrated in psychological research. We stabilize each other through our responsiveness such that negative reactions can actually deaden a person's neurological functioning for that time when the reaction is present. Partners unfortunately frequently shut each other down in this way. If one person has wounds around sex, for instance, over time his or her partner learns not to try to engage sexually because of the feeling of rejection that ensues. The partner may even stop having sexual feelings toward the beloved, and may even forget certain options and avenues in life exist that would otherwise be a natural part of his or her thinking process.

Or, perhaps one person has a passionate, outgoing side, but it overwhelms the other person and causes him or her to withdraw. The passionate part of the person may then become subdued or seemingly dead. I believe the passion can always be re-awakened, though it might take work because it has been trained that no place exists in which it can be accepted and enjoyed. When people lose parts of themselves because of how that part is received, they often become depressed or experience a sense of loss or emptiness. Rescuing and reclaiming these aspects of ourselves enlivens our spirits and allows us to have more energy and clarity. You can do this work through the healing process described in the chapter on healing yourself. If you feel you have squelched a part of your beloved, you can help this aspect resurface by responding positively to it whenever you see a tiny hint of it shining through, encouraging it to come out more.

It is, of course, easier to prevent losing aspects of each other in the first place by paying attention to where you close off and why—seeking healing rather than acting out in a way that will train your beloved towards his or her lesser self. Just as I found that most classes at two universities contained at least a handful of students who appeared very excited to learn from me and that focusing on these students inspired me to teach a dynamic and engaging class, if you nod, smile, make eye contact, and show genuine excitement about what people have to offer, you will bring out their best and create more interesting conversations and experiences. Actively engaging your positive attention on your partner means that you get to enjoy his or her best self that you have invited to emerge.

Consistently responding with a certain level of interest and caring is part of respect and basic politeness, but its power to nurture and maintain a healthy relationship is astounding. From there, you can increase your level of positive response when your beloved does or says something that is meaningful to you or which you would like to have happen more frequently. Our brains are clever enough that without ever becoming conscious of the learning process that has occurred, we will increase behaviors that lead to positive outcomes or to receiving things we need or want. Now, this process of changing a partner's behavior through reinforcement may seem degrading or manipulative, and perhaps it is if seen as a way of "training" someone. However, these principles are at work in your relationship whether or not you are conscious of them, and do have a powerful impact on who we are with various people. Awareness of how these psychological processes work can at least ensure that you are not unknowingly undermining your relationship with the way you currently respond to your beloved.

Many people I see in couple's therapy, for instance, actually respond negatively to receiving what they desire from their beloveds, causing the beloved to stop giving it. For instance, many times I see one person compliment the other or make a relationship-affirming statement, and the other person just stares back at him or her blankly, or even takes it as an opportunity to state more complaints. This response decreases the likelihood that the beloved will want to try that again! On a spiritual level, we all need love and encouragement anyway. If we do not give these gifts to the people we love, especially when they are trying or doing something deserving of acknowledgement, it seems our spirits suffer as much as those around us. The powerful effects of reinforcement merely point to the deep need we have for love, which should flow through us to others increasingly freely as we grow and connect with the Source of Goodness.

So, really drink from what your beloved gives you and that will encourage more of the same. Every relationship has difficult aspects and places for improvement, but rather than give these places all your energy and focus (though they may seem to demand it), acknowledge and strengthen the beautiful parts. Always remember why you fell in love with this person and keep your eyes on these qualities. If you appreciate where the two of you connect and really soak up the experience of these places, they may feed your spirit more than you thought. Because we all face so many obstacles when we enter into such an intimate long-term partnership, remembering Love and bringing it out becomes vital in preserving and deepening that caring, and allows fulfillment and peace to hold and heal the conflicts that we will naturally face. In other words, do not allow the little loving touches, pet names, or small gestures of care, to go unnoticed. Instead open your heart as fully as you can and let the quality of the Love in that moment pour in and nurture you. Always find the Love and give yourself to It.

Banishing Boredom

Many couples find that at different points in the relationship they feel bored. Some even leave marriages because of boredom. Boredom is simply a sign that the relationship needs to go deeper. If you are so comfortable at the level of intimacy you have that you become bored, it is time to take the next step forward in the relationship—it is NOT an excuse to back away instead. Relationships, just like the psyche or heart of an individual, are infinitely complex. You can never reach a point where new territory to explore is not unfolding if you are willing to travel there. Sometimes boredom has an element of hostility. Most people have dead places inside that they expect someone else to make come alive, causing anger when the other person cannot provide that stimulation. Instead of feeling the anger or working on enlivening the parts inside themselves that need it, they become bored and think the relationship is to blame.

Boredom seems related to a defense that we have not yet discussed. Earlier we talked about "fight or flight," defenses that evolved when we had to be prepared to run from a bear or fight another animal to protect ourselves or get food, so when the body thinks we are in an emergency situation it sends all of our blood to our large muscles, and away from the brain and digestive system. Two more survival defenses we can add to that list are "freeze" and "friendly." My mentor at Middlebury College, Andrea Olsen, described these in her book, Body and Earth. People do not only fight or flee, we also freeze as deer or rabbits do when they are in danger. Many people today have digestive trouble or tight muscles that manifest from stress (the modern day threatening situation) because they are not breathing deeply or allowing enough movement inside to circulate the body's fluids—they freeze inside. Many clients describe wishing they would disappear, and in session they are so still they almost look frozen. Their approach to safety was preventing attack by not being noticed. Boredom seems to fall under this defense. We have chosen to stand still in life and have become emotionally bored.

The "friendly" defense occurs when we use our smile or words to keep people away rather than to invite them in or communicate. It evolved early on when apes would grimace (today's smile—raising the edges of the mouth) at each other as a way of saying: "I won't hurt you. Don't hurt me." Today the smile can express real love, but many times we still use it as the apes did. Our quick, smiling: "How are you?", "Great!", seems to speak more of protection from conflict or real connection than it does of true caring. I'm sure you know people whose "false self" or "social self" is impossible to penetrate. You will never really know them—and they may not know themselves—so they are perfectly protected within a shell of niceties. Some people talk so quickly or forcefully that they do not seem to feel what they are saying—another way of preventing oneself from real relationship or emotions. I had a friend in college who was talking a mile a minute about something difficult. I

WATER YOUR TREE

interrupted when she slipped in: "I can't stand it anymore." I asked her to stop and say that to me again, but slowly, making eye-contact, and taking a breath. Suddenly a throwaway sentence that she probably did not even know she said, became her gateway to knowing herself. As she slowed down and spoke the words again, she began to cry.

Andrea encountered the "friendly" defense when traveling alone in her early twenties. A man in a tall black hat followed her up to her room and put his foot in the door when she tried to close it. He forced his way into her room and locked the door behind him. She began talking extremely quickly with no breaks, going on and on: "It's because of people like you that people like me have to be afraid...." Eventually, he just left. She could not have run, or successfully fought, or held still enough to go unnoticed, so when her defenses took over she was able to keep someone away through talking. It is not what she said, but the impenetrable energy and strength that existed in the string of sentences with no room to get in edgewise. She created a wall with words. It is important in relationships to think about whether you are talking to communicate or to keep people away. The friendly defense can also lead to boredom because it blocks the authentic connection between two people, preventing the excitement and fulfillment that real intimacy creates.

In addition to boredom providing a call for deepening, and possibly an opportunity to address one's anger that others do not ignite the places inside that are frozen—that one has to do that oneself—boredom can also be a sign of

AWAKEN TO LOVE

<u>not enough contact or needs being met outside the relationship.</u> Relationships need fresh material, ideas, and experiences. It is impossible to have all of one's needs met by one relationship. Look to others to bring freshness to your relationship by including them in the picture. Have double dates, nights with friends, and company for dinner. If you and your beloved regularly go your separate ways for a day or evening, you bring back new insights, perspectives, and stories to share that enrich the relationship. If you get together with friends as a couple, you are able to see new aspects of your beloved that are brought out by various groups of friends. You are able to deepen the relationship through knowing different parts of each other as they naturally emerge with new stimuli. This process is vital in keeping a relationship exciting and preventing symbiosis. Not bringing outside influence and material into the relationship can be an invitation for stagnation and boredom. Two people simply cannot meet all of each other's needs.

Allowing yourself to be dynamic and always growing also gives life to your relationship. Many people get caught in a need for control, which can lead to rigidity and a feeling of being alone (no room exists for collaboration when you have to be in complete control). Allowing your beloved to influence you is a powerful way to show you love him or her. You sacrifice some control—not doing something how you would have without his or her input—but you gain life-giving flexibility and a sense of togetherness with another. As we all to some degree play out with our partners the relationships we had with our parents, rebellion and even doing something the opposite of how a partner prefers can creep into a relationship if you allow it. We not only sacrifice peacefulness and upset our households by staunchly doing things our way just to protect our sense of selves, but miss the opportunity to make our partners feel special by showing them they are important enough for us to change little things (sometimes meaningless things such as where we take off our shoes when we come in the house!) for them. This dynamic is also important in parenting. If you are with the children and have lost your temper and your partner comes in and suggests you go into the other room and let him or her handle the situation: say yes! Allowing yourself to be influenced, or even letting your partner take over, especially when he or she is more sane at the moment, is all a part of teamwork—not weakness.

The Role of Ritual

Another way of deepening your relationship and making it feel more meaningful is to incorporate ritual or ceremony into your life. Create a sacred space that makes it easier for your mind and heart to leave the mundane and focus on a deeper level of communion together. For some, an environment that invites holiness or contemplation of the Essence is nature. A walk holding hands every day at sunset might be a meaningful ritual that anchors you to the realm where your heart can really be fed. For others, lighting candles might evoke that sense of significance that encourages going beyond the everyday. Perhaps you and your beloved eat dinner, just the two of you, by candlelight once a week or make love by candlelight with the intention of really knowing each other more fully. Reading poetry about nature or love tends to create a sacred space. The key is knowing what kind of situation best fits you and your beloved. Perhaps, for you, regularly attending a baseball game and cheering on a team together facilitates closeness and a sense of meaning. You can add further significance to these moments by drawing attention to them and commenting on them: "Last year it was raining during the third game of the season, remember? I almost slipped on the way into the stadium and then we were laughing throughout the whole game! I love doing this with you year after year."

These special times can be as intimate as you can imagine. Perhaps you and your beloved are already so connected that your deepening time would be looking into each other's eyes without speaking for an hour, just feeling how your hearts respond to each other and dance together. For most, a wonderful step would be simply adding a minute-long hug or a 3-second kiss and a 3-second eye contact when coming back together at the end of each day. In any case, the purpose is to increase spirit and meaning, taking yourself out of the "rat in a maze" feeling that characterizes today's society, and reminding yourself of what is important—allowing the heart connection to flower and feeling the Divine in your relationship and in your life.

You may sometimes feel the need for a more formal ceremony. I have performed recommitment ceremonies for my friends where I hold the space for them to renew their

WATER YOUR TREE

vows or to tell each other what they mean to each other. What makes a ceremony different from just telling each other casually in the kitchen? Both are lovely, of course, but a ceremony tends to be more profound and make a greater impact because of sacred space and intention. Creating an environment that feels special and beautiful facilitates your truly opening your heart and being fully present, while the intention to do something outside of the ordinary seems to shift the level at which our beings respond to what is happening. One couple got dressed up, bought flowers, lit candles, and had me read some love poetry as they looked into each other's eyes. Then, they shared their commitments with each other to fight less, to start fresh, to take care of each other's hearts, and to be there for each other no matter what. Ceremonies seem to solidify whatever is being honored and make it more real.

    I remember when I first started planning my wedding. I am not one who enjoys shopping and spending large amounts of time in the superficial world making choices about which earrings to wear, etc. However, I realized early on that the more time I spent planning the wedding, the more real it was to me that I was going to be married. I began to see the year of wedding planning as a ceremony in itself. The understanding that I was starting a new family and making a life-long commitment sank in more with every flower color and song I chose. This ritual of the planning process brought me to a place in my heart where by the time I said, "I do," I already felt married—it was no longer an idea in my mind, but a reality in my psyche and soul.

AWAKEN TO LOVE

My sister and her husband had talked a lot about becoming engaged before they did so. Since they both already knew it was coming, they decided to think of a ceremony so that their engagement would still be special and memorable. They sat next to each other on pillows with 5 rows of three candles before them. Each row represented one year that they had been together. First they each stated their favorite memories from that year and lit the first candle in that row. Then they talked about what challenges they overcame that year and what they learned from them, and lit the second candle in that row. Then, they each said how they saw the other person that year and what they came to appreciate about who the other person is, and lit the third candle. They took time doing each year this way, traveling through the whole relationship and the unfolding and blossoming of their love. They ended by telling each other that they wanted to be together forever.

==I invite you to see how you can add more meaning and special moments to your daily life and to your relationship through ceremony, ritual, or some other way that moves your heart.== Perhaps it would be enough to simply add a toast from time to time when you sit down with your orange juice or cocoa in the morning, gently raising your glass with your beloved and whispering: "To us."

I wonder if the vulnerability in such a moment would make it difficult for many people to allow themselves to initiate. I could imagine someone dismissing anything that involves an uncomfortable amount of closeness as "cheesy." Vulnerability, however, seems a key ingredient in intimacy, or at least powerfully facilitates it in a loving context. Therefore, if you want more connection and meaning in your relationship, look at what blocks you from vulnerability. Usually the barriers are wounds waiting to be healed. Perhaps vulnerability is merely an open heart—and who would choose a life without that? We do not choose what closed our hearts in the first place, but we can always choose to do the work to open them again. Yes, past injuries might make it scary, but do not stop with the fear. Beyond it you might find your true self, longing to be known.

Your spiritual perspective is vital in moving pictures and voices from past wounds. Fear is merely an invitation to go deeper with God and find the security in your own being that no one can take away from you. From a place of safety and strength as you bathe in the Divine qualities, you may feel more willing to be vulnerable on the outside and allow the beauty within to be brought into relationship with the outer world, because you know nothing is at stake. The outer vulnerability is a mere veil and behind it you are complete and sufficed no matter how an outside interaction transpires. Every moment you do not feel this security from the outer world is a wonderful gift, acting as a gentle reminder to go inside and drink from Love. Do not deny or push away any discomfort you have as you allow an increasing amount of intimacy in your relationship. Instead, say "yes" to the experience of discomfort or any other feeling you are having. Accept, feel, and face it deeply, and then open further to feel God's perspective on the situation and see how the Divine is moving in that moment. What are you being reminded to receive from your true Beloved? Once you feel how God relates to you in this place, fill your cup to overflowing.

Your Inner Male & Female

With vulnerability, or any quality with which you want to become more comfortable, you may consider your inner male and female and the relationship between the two. Though we have a gender on the outer, inside we are a complex mix of qualities, some of which are more feminine and some more masculine. It is important to observe how you hold these qualities so that you can come into balance and versatility as you grow spiritually. Perhaps your masculine side is over-developed because growing up you had to be strong to protect your siblings from one of your parents. Or maybe your mother did not know how to relate to your father, or even to her own masculine side, so to be in relationship with her you had to disown your masculine qualities and be all feminine. Whatever your story, each of us has preferences in terms of the qualities with which we lead, as in a language in which we are most fluent. To be complete, we can develop choice about how we respond to our environments and be able to immerse ourselves in any of God's qualities as the Divine moves us in each moment, whether that means being soft and nurturing or strong and directive—compassionate or wise.

You may also consider how the masculine and feminine in you relate to each other. Sometimes we have internalized the relationship between our parents or the relationship between men and women that was modeled for us growing up. Many healing traditions say the right side of the body tends to be the masculine and the left side is the feminine. So, if that is a useful way of visualizing it for you, you can sit in Remembrance and feel how the two sides of your body interact and how they feel about each other. Otherwise, simply notice how you feel about your masculine and feminine parts and you will begin to understand the relationship they have with each other inside.

For instance, if every time you start to feel tender or gentle you become tight and scared, or you criticize yourself for being weak, then you see how the masculine side of you rules the feminine and scares that part of you or shames it away. If you are a woman whose own masculine side is shutting down the feminine, tolerating a man in your life who does the same thing will be even more difficult and hurtful, as we project all the pain we feel from this internal dynamic onto our outer relationships. Perhaps, instead, the feminine side rules inside you and tells the masculine aspects that if they come out they will get you into trouble or physical danger (maybe standing up to dad led to physical danger as a child, for instance), or cause rejection (if strength and competence were not rewarded growing up, but instead you had to please everyone). These dynamics in you and in your partner can greatly affect the power and nurturance in the relationship and how the flow of giving and receiving happens, or does not happen.

Perhaps your own dominant aspects need to give those qualities to your less dominant side to support that part of you in coming out and creating more balance in your life. One or both facets of you may need healing work to clean the skewed version of those qualities and bring them into the holiness of their potential. For instance, if your masculine side is domineering, you can clean it into true strength, which contains love, flexibility, and the capacity to surrender or lead with clarity and ease. Or maybe your feminine side has difficulty setting boundaries and gives until you resent it or burn out. The generosity and patience in you could be cleaned to be in alignment with real guidance so that you would know when to give and how to say no. Is the real nurturance to take care of everyone indiscriminately so that you will be liked, or to model taking care of yourself and then giving love generously in the way your wisdom shows you that people really need, even if it is not what they want? As you explore your masculine and feminine sides, and their relationships to God, you will find the answers in your heart to these kinds of questions that point the way toward balance and wholeness.

Layers of the Heart

We have been discussing the relationship between your own inner aspects, now let's shift to the relationship between the layers of your heart and the layers of your beloved's heart. We can look at our whole being as having layers that deepen until at our deepest we are in Unity, God-Realization,

Christ-Consciousness, Enlightenment, Completion, or whatever your spiritual path or religion calls our arrival in God. We can call these levels the "layers of the heart" because they seem to be mapped into the heart center from the outer level toward the front of your chest to the deeper places in your heart as you move inward toward your back.

The Sufis, whose spiritual path focuses on falling in love with God, are experts on the heart. Their mystical conceptualization is useful in understanding the different levels of how we relate to our beloveds. They describe the outer-most layer as the self, personality, or ego. It operates in attachment to the physical world and to fulfilling its needs. Beneath that is the heart layer of the heart. The heart level is where the deeper emotions move. It tends to hold more Truth, but can also be hurt and have feelings that come from reaction to injuries rather than its innate wisdom. It seems to turn back and forth between attachment to the world and attachment to God. For the most part, however, the heart is generous and holds the potential for unconditional love and compassion, as it naturally longs to give and receive caring. The soul is the third layer of the heart. This level is closer to witnessing Love, but still has its individuality that separates it from another soul. Here is where God's qualities move through people as light. Through our life experiences, even our souls can turn away from Love to various degrees, and the way the Divine qualities manifest in us can be muted or covered over. Yet, this level is still more subtle, holy, and close to God.

So, all of the first three levels of the heart need purification as we go through this life, returning again and again to alignment with God, and cleaning the mirror of our existence so that we reflect back the Divine in everything. The fourth, and deepest, layer of the heart is called the secret. It is secret because you have to discover it to know it. Everyone has this deepest layer where we lose our individual self and can only identify with God. It is subtle and sacred, yet more Real than anything else we experience because this level is the fabric of everything in existence. We feel Unity with all of creation and experience our own Divine essence. Many religions hold that God lives in people's hearts. The secret level is this home, where no separation exists between us and the One.

We can choose to live our lives from any of these levels. It takes most people some seeking before they find the jewel inside where they know their true selves at the deepest level. If you take some time to do Remembrance and place your hand on your heart, you can practice feeling the different levels of your being and understanding from where you are operating in each moment, as well as who you are at each level. A lot of our experiences in daily life have to do with which part of ourselves we are witnessing. I remember times when I was angry at my husband and told him about it, for instance, and he asked me how my deeper heart felt about it. In about five seconds he would help me sink back into the soul level of my heart and I would feel such stillness and peace that I could not find the issue about which I had been upset. Very tricky of him!! Those times are my most tangible experience of how each layer of my being has its own reality and holds its own issues. As an aside, the process I described did not heal the anger, it simply took me into another room of the house than the room in which the anger lived. In healing, as described previously, you sit in the room the issue is in, experience it as fully and directly as possible, and then allow God to meet you there.

So that you can recognize each layer, I'll say more about how they might feel. The self contains many voices, telling you to stop your exploration and go do something related to the outer world and your ego's connection with it. The self is concerned with managing your life. Maybe you are a list-maker, or pine over what needs to happen in your job, relationship, family, etc. Maybe your self wants to go eat, have sex, read, listen to music, swim, manage your budget, work out or whatever your self likes and does to gain its sense of well-being and safety. Some desires of the self are healthy and some destructive, but either way they tend to take you into the world of things rather than the spiritual world. When you are in the self you feel attached to things being a certain way. Once you sink into the heart layer you feel more internal and discerning because you are more connected with the truth of who you are.

The heart is a more experiential landscape where your mind is no longer in control, but instead your heart is revealing things to you organically. You may feel emotions, places where you were hurt or are longing. The heart level is full and rich. It is the part that gives you that felt sense of the world that we call intuition, or guidance. The soul level, in contrast, often feels airy or spacious because it is much larger than the body and less attached to the physical world. In this space you may feel a quiet stillness or sense of expansion. Things feel less personal and less emotional—more calm and spiritual. It can feel completely empty and full at the same time. In the soul you understand your spiritual nature and purpose. The secret layer of the heart is where you lose yourself altogether and the drop returns to the ocean. You are not concerned with your experience anymore because all that exists is God.

So, how do you and your beloved relate at each of these levels? We can look at this question from a base level and from an everyday level. In a basic way, the levels of people's hearts seem to have an innate response to each other. Two people may meet and their "selves" like each other because they have so much in common and fit each other's needs and pictures (who the self imagined it was looking for). Or perhaps the selves are attracted to each other's appearance. Perhaps their hearts accept each other, but are not necessarily ignited. At the soul level, however, perhaps the souls do not mesh well or for some reason repel each other. Between the apathy of the hearts' relationship and the distance in the souls, the couple may feel a lack of spark or something substantive that they may or may not be able to name. Such a couple could still be passionate if the selves are madly in love and if the two people tend to live from this outer level of reality.

Others describe finding their soul mate. These are the relationships where the soul levels of the people are so drawn

WATER YOUR TREE

to each other that they are like one soul. Sometimes their selves may not get along. Whether or not these relationships work out can depend on how able the couple is to continue living from their deeper hearts, and how much a couple can clean their outer selves to be less attached to having things a certain way. Ideally, in a long-term relationship, all layers of the hearts are at least somewhat compatible and satisfied with each other, but many couples have some levels that are easier for them to relate in than others.

On a more everyday level, you can feel how the different layers of your heart relate to those of your beloved in any moment. As you take time to feel your heart and travel deeper into it so that you explore the levels we described, you can look out (with the eye of the heart) from each layer at the corresponding layer in your beloved and feel how you relate to him or her from this place. You might find that from the level of the self you are trying so hard to care for your beloved and he or she is demanding more, but when you look from your heart level your beloved's heart is crying for more attention from you because your heart is turned away. So, in this case, a heart-level dynamic manifested at a more outer level, but was misleading because it looked as though you were giving everything on the outside, when inside your heart rejected your beloved. No wonder he or she was floundering and lonely. Of course, the number of dynamics that could be playing out among these layers of your and your beloved's beings is limitless. To discover the truth of the relationship from a spiritual perspective, however, it is vital to take time to sit and feel what is happening in the deeper levels.

Without taking time to sit in silence and feel these places, you may also simply notice from where you or your beloved are communicating in any given conversation. If you hear from yourself or your beloved (or both) a lot of complaining about worldly things and ruminating about how the partner should be different and meet one's outer needs more fully, one is witnessing the self. This outer personality operates from expectations of your beloved to satisfy your desires, and therefore a typical statement from it might include: "I want" or "I need you to…." The heart, in contrast, longs to serve and love, so its statement might be more along the lines of "How can I enrich your life?" Even when hurt, it speaks more in the language of: "I feel…."

Very few couples live in the soul enough to communicate from this level without consciously going to this place. Because the soul sees the real essence of the other person and appreciates its beauty, this level might say: "Your being is so beautiful. I'm so grateful to be in this relationship." At the secret level partners cannot distinguish between one another, but only experience God. At this level, with no separation, only Love exists in the relationship. Over time you can develop choice about from which of these layers to operate. You may be able to deepen an interchange with your partner from the surface to the real heart—a much more productive and potentially healing place from which to communicate. As mentioned, we can also look at what our beloveds need at each layer of their beings so that we can give the true medicine, and not get caught in the idea that what they are showing us is the complete picture of who they are.

When I first met my husband he was difficult for me on the outer level because we are so different in our communication styles and our views of the world. Yet, when we said good-bye for the first time (we met at a conference and traveled back to our respective homes afterward) I felt a profound sadness and longing come over me—as though part of me was leaving. This feeling shows how immediate my soul connection with him was. I believe it was our souls' similarity and merging that held us together through the difficult work of learning to love each other in a way in which we could both be happy, yet still grow. Several spiritual teachers independently told us that my husband offers me an enormous well of unconditional love, but that it comes at a deeper level of my being than the one in which I lived at the time. I offered him an outpouring of love from the self and the heart, but was less present in the deeper levels in which he prefers to reside.

We both gave at the level on which we wished to receive, but not at the level that was most accessible to the other person. Through my developing my inner world and connection to the more subtle realms, while he focused on bringing his love all the way through to manifest more overtly in the outer world, we have both developed spiritually while at the same time creating a deeply fulfilling relationship. Though he now does the little things for me that make me feel loved, I have not lost the chance to experience the beauty of his natural way of giving. Just recently we were hugging and I felt something I had never felt. It was a subtle, yet powerful, expansive love for me from a much deeper place in him than I had ever been able to experience. I soaked it in and tried to bathe in that nectar as deeply as I could. I felt myself able to give to him at that level too. From the outside the hug was just like any of our other hugs, but when we let go and looked into each other's eyes, he was teary. ==I knew he had felt that I was finally meeting him where he had been longing to be with me.==

To close, I would like to tell a story that illustrates the soul and secret-level connection. Both the grandparents of one of my best friends had Alzheimer's disease a few years ago, one for nine years and one for five. They lived down the hall from each other in a nursing home with no contact between them or recognition of each other, despite having had a long (fifty years!) and loving marriage previous to their dementia. My friend reported that one day her grandfather wheeled himself to his wife's room, to her bedside, and took her hand. He held it all day. The nurses sensed the importance of the moment, later describing to my friend the way the couple gazed into each other's eyes without a word. The nurses brought in a bed so that he could sleep in her room. He slept there that night and she died the next day.

A knowing exists that is beyond the mind, which in this case was profoundly deteriorated. This understanding moved the grandfather to seek out his soul mate, whose name he no longer knew, because she was leaving, which he seemed to have intuited. The connection between people goes deeper than words, deeper than this reality, and deeper than the ability to think. It is a profound interweaving of hearts, souls, and secrets that is perhaps more able than any other aspect of creation, in its beauty and pain, to point us toward the all-encompassing mystery, Oneness, and tender love of the Divine.

[i] The Meadow of Poetic Truths. Shaykh Muhammad Said al-Jamal ar-Rifa'I as-Shadhuli. Sidi Muhammad Press: Petaluma, CA, 2001, p. 145-147.
[ii] Harlow, H. F. (1973) Learning to Love. Oxford, England: Ballantine.
[iii] Siegel, D. (1999). The developing mind: How relationships and the brain interact to shape who we are. New York: Guilford Press.
Siegel, D. (2001). Toward an interpersonal neurobiology of the developing mind: Attachment relationships, "mindsight," and neural integration. *Infant Mental Health Journal, 22*, 67-94.
Siegel, D. (2003). Attachment and self-understanding: Parenting with the brain in mind. In M. Green & M. Scholes (Eds.), Attachment and Human Survival. New York: Karnac Books.
[iv] Joseph, R. (1999). Environmental influences on neural plasticity, the limbic system, emotional development and attachment: A review. *Child Psychiatry and Human Development, 19*(3), 189-206.
[v] Schore, A. (2002). Dysregulation of the right brain: A fundamental mechanism of traumatic attachment and the psychopathogenesis of posttraumatic stress disorder. *Australian and New Zealand Journal of Psychiatry, 36*, 9-30.
[vi] Presentation by Walter E. Brackelmanns, M.D. at the American Group Psychotherapy Conference in Austin, 2007.
[vii] Conversations in the Zowiyah. Sidi Shaykh Muhammad Said al-Jamal ar-Rifa'i. Sidi Muhammad Press: Petaluma, CA, 1999, p. 24-26.
[viii] Music of the Soul. Shaykh Muhammad Said al-Jamal ar-Rifa'I as-Shadhuli. Sidi Muhammad Press: Petaluma, CA, 1994, p. 172, 171-172.
[ix] Yvonne Agazarian's System's Centered Theory®.
[x] Dr. Robert Jaffe of the University of Spiritual Healing and Sufism
[xi] Walking with God. James Keeley. Rosewood Press: Berkeley Springs, WV, 2006.
[xii] Music of the Soul. Shaykh Muhammad Said al-Jamal ar-Rifa'I as-Shadhuli. Sidi Muhammad Press: Petaluma, CA, 1994, p. 171-172.
[xiii] Yvonne Agazarian's work on sub-grouping in her System's Centered Theory®.
[xiv] Yvonne Agazarian's System's Centered Theory®
[xv] Yvonne Agazarian's System's Centered Theory®
[xvi] Yvonne Agazarian's System's Centered Theory®
[xvii] Yvonne Agazarian's System's Centered Theory®
[xviii] The following four paragraphs are based on the work of Walter E. Brackelmanns, M.D., as presented at the American Group Psychotherapy Association's annual conference in Austin, TX, March 10, 2007.
[xix] Yvonne Agazarian's System's Centered Theory®